To Catheri…



Be blessed as you …
Your Inner Treasure!

8/26/07

# Releasing Your *Inner* Treasure

## 8 Kingdom Keys to Unlocking the Wealth Within You

DR. TECOY M. PORTER, SR.

FOGHORN
PUBLISHERS
"Of Making Many Books There Is No End . . ."

**Releasing Your Inner Treasure**: *8 Kingdom Keys To Unlocking The Wealth Within You*

ISBN-13: 978-1-934466-01-8
ISBN-10: 1-934466-01-8

Genesis Church
2801 Meadowview Road
Sacramento, CA 95683
(916) 422-8772
www.sacgenesis.org

Foghorn Publishers
P.O. Box 8286
Manchester, CT 06040-0286
860-216-5622
860-568-4821 FAX
foghornpublisher@aol.com

*In memory of my loving parents*

*Dr. Robert Porter and Mrs. Hazel R. Porter*

# *Dedication*

One never truly understands the impact a project will have on his life in its infancy. The impact is always more than originally anticipated: more time, more money, more "no's and not yet's"—especially to family. So I must first thank my family for allowing my time away from them throughout the years while working on this great undertaking. I already know I have wrestling matches to make up, and a number of other activities to catch up with. Special thanks to my wife, Karlette, who was my first proofreader, editor and sounding board. Thanks for your undying support. Thanks for enduring this journey with me! We were truly designed for each other.

To my brother, Ellington Porter, you are more than my sibling, but my friend. Thank you for your constant encouragement and excitement towards my dreams. We are an unbeatable team! The best is yet to come!

To my Genesis Church staff, thank you for believing in me, and in my innovative approach to pastoring. Your effectiveness has allowed me to focus on being the best I can be and has allowed me to complete this book. Because of you that I know— Teamwork makes The Dream work!

To my Genesis Church Family, you are a very special church. Before we knew each other, God connected us together. Your undying love and loyalty has allowed my family and me to reach heights we've never dreamed of. This book is especially for you. I can hardly wait to see what the future has in store for us.

To my West and East Coast fathers: DJ Rogers and Bishop Sam Williams. I thank God for your wisdom, encouragement, optimism, guidance and covering. Words cannot express how much you have helped me throughout the years. Know that I am forever grateful.

To Deneen Brown, editor, thank you for showing your Pastor favor. You were the answer to my prayers. I look forward to seeing you on Oprah!

Finally, I thank God for my life and this wonderful journey. I'll be the first to admit that I haven't always understood every aspect of the journey, but I now realize that everything I went through was working towards my greater good. I trust you completely and pray that you are pleased with me.

# *Foreword*

It seems as if I have read immense numbers of books on prosperity written by preachers. Although I do not have any problem with preachers writing books on this topic, few if any of them, really had lasting depth in their works. Many of the books dealt with sowing the seed to receive a financial harvest. As truthful as that message is, it is only a part of the much larger scheme of things when dealing with money.

It's somewhat like teaching young major leaguers about the importance of getting to first base, yet never stressing the importance of hitting a home run. Much of the body of Christ is still waiting on first base without any idea what else they should do. Sowing the seed is really the initial step, one that millions have yet to cross. However, for those of us who have already conquered step number one, we desperately wait with patience for our next marching orders.

Other writers write from a pompous perspective, making the Average Joe feel like a total schmuck if they haven't reached the heights of the elite society. Then you have a group of people who are totally anti-prosperity all together. They believe that it is not God's will for His children to have and enjoy big money, since money has the potential to contaminate good manners, so they say. This group is perhaps the most lethal of all.

They parade around under the guise of humility and holiness, yet their hearts are far from God, and their understanding of Biblical interpretation lacks miserably. They say things such as, "The devil wants to make you rich so that you will turn your heart away from God." Nonsense. If that were really true, the devil wouldn't even try to tempt anyone to sin. He'd simply make all of God's children rich; load them with money beyond their imagination so they will turn their hearts away from God. For the most part people who talk that way are only making excuses for why they've lived life so pathetically, never tapping into their optimal self. The bottom line is that we desperately need balance.

Of the many books that I have read and reviewed I have finally found one that I can honestly say provides the balanced approach to financial prosperity. One of the things that I appreciate about this work is that it is not pretentious in the least bit. Every word comes from the heart of a man who has a sincere desire to see the Body of Christ leading in every area, which also includes the area of finances. Our churches lead in musical expertise. We lead in the area of preaching prowess. And no one on earth can praise the Lord like a Holy Ghost filled believer. Sadly we fall at the bottom of the totem pole when it comes to financial management. That must change!

Porter is a man of means. He is well established and has a good financial perspective. If he so desired he could have easily taken the route of your average prosperity preacher and dealt solely with the seed theory. Porter could have also taken the approach of the others who say, "I've got the goods and if you want them, listen to me, stupid." Instead Porter chose the road least traveled, the road, which required him to simply follow his heart. Written in the style of a loving father talking to his aspiring son, Dr. Tecoy Porter opens up his heart and tells his story in a most special way, of how he personally came to understand the principles that govern wealth.

Porter believes that if God used him to be a financial conduit, a money missionary if you will, that He could use virtually anybody. All it takes to become wealthy is just a little adjustment in a few areas, and a tenacious dedication to embrace and follow hard after each kingdom key that Porter so articulately laid out in this book. Releasing Your Inner Treasure: 8 Kingdom Keys To Unlocking The Wealth Within You is a very unique work in that it identifies the problem yet quickly offers the solution, something that few books do today. It takes you on a journey of discovery of self, the self that you never met before.

You will learn that you've always had within you the potential and possibility to become one of the richest persons on earth, if not the richest. Everything that you need is already within you. That, you will discover. But you will also discover how powerful and underrated money really is. Money is not only power. Money is freedom. It can buy positions, influence, and it can bring about promotion as well. Never underestimate the power of money.

While this book mentions money and teaches you why believers need to control the dollar, it also deals with the most valuable and precious commodity on earth, YOU. You are worth more than any dollar amount, yet for so long you were a servant of something that is beneath you, money. You were created to have dominion. You should control money, not the other way around. Porter shares many personal testimonies that I am sure will benefit and intrigue every reader.

If you want to get to the top in life, let Dr. Porter show you how to get there. While most of the people in society desire to get rich quick, Porter shows us how to get rich a totally different way, using one kingdom key at a time. Here is the master key, turn each page, read it in its entirety, until the book is finished. After that, review what you have read, then apply the principles to your life. Then you just might be ready to meet face-to-face, the wealth trapped within. The power to get wealth is not elusive neither is it an ethereal reality. The power to get wealth rest in the same place that it has always been inside of you, waiting to come out.

> *Now to Him who is able to do exceedingly abundantly above all that we ask or think, according to the power that works in us, to Him be glory in the church by Christ Jesus to all generations, forever and ever. Amen.* Ephesians 3:20-21NKJV

**Aaron D. Lewis, Ph.D.**
The Family of God, Glastonbury, CT
Author, *Keys To Unlocking Your Destiny*

# *Table of Contents*

# Introduction

With all of the information on wealth building, prosperity and obtaining riches in both secular and sacred circles, you may wonder why I took the time to write another book on the subject. The answer to this question is simple—there's still a need. There is still a need to learn the truth about obtaining wealth God's way, especially within the body of Christ. Throughout history the subject of money has been considered taboo in most churches. With the rising number of prosperity teachers who focus on the financial well being of Christians, many leaders have become gun-shy to teach about giving offerings, tithing, and other financial matters.

Consequently, generations upon generations of God's children have suffered in a state of poverty and mediocrity their entire lives. Living from paycheck to paycheck, depending upon government assistance, hardly able to make ends meet, have become a commonplace for most believers. Sad to say that the only legacy that most people leave to their children, is debt and shattered dreams. Church leaders being silent on this issue, has really taken its toll on the people they serve. Christian marriages now hold the highest divorce rate among all marriages in America, sighting money as its primary reason.

Instead of congregations filled with families of two parents households, single parent victims of "dysfunctional families," now fill the pews. Many families struggle to keep their hopes alive in a world filled with doubt and dismay. What this does to the mission of the church is nearly catastrophic. Instead of the church being a beacon of light in their communities, they are contributors to the depravity of their neighborhood. Unfortunately, churches are just struggling to survive, trying to keep the lights on and members in the pews. Much of this can be attributed to their own resistance to change.

Many members are more concerned with their own financial welfare than the mission of God's Kingdom. That thinking really defeats the purpose of the church. This statement may sound cold, but how else can one explain a community full of churches, *large and small,* on every corner, yet experiencing little to no change socially or economically. Where is the transforming power of the church in our communities? Why are these communities still plagued with drugs, gangs, poverty, and pollution? Why are these churches and their leaders being overlooked when it comes to civic decisions affecting their communities? Why do some churches seem to be irrelevant to present day society? The answer is: these churches have no power! And the reason they have no power is because they have no money!

## The Answer

*Money answereth all things.* —Ecclesiastes 10:19b

King Solomon, who was considered the wisest man who ever lived, said that money answers all things— and he was right. In our society, money does answer all things. Money, when used properly, will give you respect, influence, and the ability to live a life of freedom. Having money allows an individual or organization to be the head and not the tail: above and not beneath: the lender and not the borrower. The tool of money allows buildings to be constructed, food and clothes to be distributed, educational goals obtained, access to media, and businesses developed.

It also allows jobs and careers to be given to the unemployed, shelter for the homeless, and big dreams realized. There really is no way of getting around it. If the church is effective in its mission of establishing God's Kingdom on earth, it must have money and plenty of it. One of the primary reasons why civic leaders overlook the majority of religious leaders *until voting time,* is because of their lack of affluence. It is hard to influence without affluence. Who wants to take advice from a poor person? Do you? The ability to produce wealth and maintain it is critical to the success of establishing God's Kingdom on earth.

Now you may be asking yourself, "What does this have to do with me?"

"What does this have to do with getting *a Millionaire Mind*?" "What does this have to do with me getting wealthy?" "I just want to learn about becoming a millionaire!"

KEEP READING! It's going to get even better.

## The Called-Out Ones

*And I say also unto thee, That thou art Peter, and upon this rock I will build my church; and the gates of hell shall not prevail against it.* —Matthew 16:18

Many people believe that the church is literally a building that they go to every Sunday, or an archaic religious institution that is separated from "the real world". Others believe the church is the choir, the ushers and deacon's board. Then there is the ever-popular thought that the church is the pastor, priest, or bishop *(who is responsible to do everything for free)*. The truth is, God never intended the church to be an archaic institution or a non-profit organization. That was man's idea. He never intended for it to be broken up into denominations, ran by boards, or defined through ministries.

Instead, God intended the church to be a living representative of His Son Jesus Christ, through the assembly of people who are linked and bound by a common belief. The church is not a building; it is a people, the gathering of the called-out ones.

According to Vine's Expository Dictionary of Old and New Testament Words the term church is derived from the Greek word *ekklesia (ek meaning "out of," and klesis, "a calling")*. The term ekklesia was often used to refer to a body of people who assembled because of a definite purpose.

When we combine both the definitions of the root words and the usage of the term, we come up with the definition of "the gathering or assembly of the called-out ones". When Christ said to Peter, "thou art Peter, and upon this rock I will build my church", he was referring prophetically to those who would gather together because they share the same revelation Peter received as Jesus being their Messiah, the Son of God. It is through this revelation they are called-out of sin, darkness and death into salvation, light and life eternal.

God's will is to establish His Kingdom on earth as it is in heaven. God's method of accomplishing this is through His church, men and women He has called out of the world to change the world. God knew we couldn't do this without possessing certain earthly attributes, so He promised us that if we seek ye first the Kingdom of God, every thing we need would be given unto us to accomplish His will, including joy, peace, happiness, health, a sound mind, and yes, even *money*.

## Who Is This Book For?

This book is for the "ekklesia", God's church. I wrote this book specifically for those who are tired of living beneath their promise, beneath their status, beneath their rights, and especially beneath their calling. This book is for those who are ready to walk into their wealthy place, now! Child of God, it is critical that you get this revelation in your spirit. The reason why the church's power has been limited is because we the believers have not fully claimed our inheritance. For far too long we have ignored the wealth of this world, which has been laid up for us by our Father in heaven. It's time for you to walk in your calling!! When Jesus saved you, He called you out of sin, death and *everything* associated with it. Some of the things associated with sins that God called you out of are:

- Poverty.
- Lack and scarcity.
- Mediocrity.

- Living from paycheck to paycheck.
- Living a life of struggling just to get by.
- Egyptian bondage mentality, believing that you never have enough.

*Thou hast caused men to ride over our heads; we went through fire and through water: but thou broughtest us out into a wealthy place.* —Psalms 66:12

God did not stop at just bringing you out, but He brought you out so you can enter your wealthy place. You must realize that your struggles, tests and trials are not in vain. Don't stop now. I'm here to help you get out into your wealthy place. You were not saved to be defeated on earth, but rather to be triumphant. God saved us to experience a foretaste here on earth of what He has prepared for us in heaven. Our salvation is not only for heaven but also for success, wealth, and health, so we will be victorious in finishing the work that He started.

# Preface

## My Story

Before you go further, I want to share with you some things about myself, and what motivated me to write this work. First, I am considered an over-achiever. I am self-motivated, driven, and very passionate at whatever I set my mind to do. Most of this is because of my upbringing and my parent's nurture and love. My father and mother, Dr. Robert Porter and Hazel Porter, gave me the infrastructure to be accomplished in many areas of my life, at an early age.

By the time I reached the age of twenty-five, I had quite an impressive resume. I traveled to many parts of the United States and Europe. I graduated from one of the most prestigious private preparatory school in the country. Many of my classmates were the sons and daughters and grandchildren of millionaire business owners, governors and senators. This exposure to the rich, continued after being accepted to the University of the Pacific's Conservatory of Music in California. There I studied music business, again along with the children and grandchildren of multi-millionaire business owners, and politicians.

Due to some financial challenges, I transferred to California State University Sacramento. There, I graduated with my Bachelors of Arts in Music and Masters of Business Administration. The very weekend after I graduated, I married my church sweetheart, Karlette. Together, along with my brother, Ellington, we started our own music production company and taught music lessons. We also produced two gospel albums for our church choir. In addition to all of this, I became an accomplished professional as a technical trainer and a project management consultant to various businesses in Northern California.

Although I wasn't the most successful guy on the planet however, I knew that I was more successful than most guys my age. In my late twenties, my family grew with the birth of my first son TJ. Our business grew into more production type work, the choir was touring nationally to support our albums, and my wife and I bought our first home in the suburbs. I moved from consulting to full time management of a highly respected technology program with the University of California System. In this position, I supervised a group of technical experts who in turn supported over 300 technical support specialists on and off campus. I was doing pretty well financially.

With all of my streams of income I was earning a six-figure income, all before the age of thirty. Around the same time that this growth was occurring, I acknowledged my call to the ministry. From the time that I was small, I always knew I would end up being a minister, as many preachers' kids do. However, I didn't quite like the notion of becoming a minister or a pastor, after witnessing first hand, the many trials I saw my father going through during his thirty plus years in the ministry. As much as I would have wanted to avoid it, I could not escape the call to ministry. It is in my blood.

### Church Boy

Even though when I was growing up, I witnessed treatment that was pretty unkind towards ministers, I did not develop negativity towards church people. I actually liked church. The fact of the matter is I am very much a church boy and have always loved being one. I gave my life to the Lord Jesus when I was five years old. I became a Junior Deacon at my dad's church around the same time. After getting tired of wayward choir directors and disloyal musicians coming and going, and also recognizing my musical potential, my father appointed me as the minister of music, *"in training"* and my brother as the church organist *"in training."*

He affixed the "in training" part to our position titles because we were so young and inexperienced. I was 15, Ellington was 12. Nonetheless, we developed into pretty good musicians and directors and became known in the community for our work with the church's music ministry. Because I was the minister of music for the church and the Pastor's eldest son, I was automatically referred to as one of the leaders in the church. This often had me leading older people, some much older than me. This was extremely beneficial as I learned many important lessons on leadership and relating with people of all ages.

Throughout my high school years, until I went off to college I held the position of music minister. I continued to help out in the Music Ministries and Deacon Boards of my father's churches even while I was in college. Looking back, I believe that my training early on as a leader is why I was able to accomplish the things that I did at an early age. As you can see, I knew a whole lot about church, so it wasn't a surprise when I announced my call to the ministry early in 1998. In May of 1998, I was licensed as a minister of the gospel. In April of 1999 my brother Ellington (who was also called to ministry a few months before me), and I were ordained and officially became my father's assistant co-pastors to the Genesis Missionary Baptist Church in Sacramento, California, which he founded in April of 1990.

## Man's Tragedy is God's Opportunity

A couple of months later, August 2, 1999, my father suddenly died at the age of 54, leaving my younger brother and I to pastor a church of more than 1200 members. My brother was 25 and I was 28. Instantly, my whole life changed. From that experience, I have learned that man's tragedy usually leads to God's opportunity. In other words, you will never experience the awesomeness of God until you have come to a point of no return. These points I like to call, Red Sea Experiences. We often fail to notice the mightiness of God until we have hit an obstacle so big that it literally prevents us from moving forward in our lives.

We can't turn around because our enemy is behind us ready to deliver the death blow. So we have no choice, but to trust God to deliver us. This is exactly what happened when the children of Israel passed over the Red Sea. We were facing an impossible situation and people were lined up just waiting to see how we were going to mess this up. If we looked at the situation as one looking in from the outside, we were two kids given this weighty responsibility of pastoring an influential and growing church in Sacramento, California.

Although we were known for our musical talents and abilities outside of the church, most people wondered if we had what it took to be the pastors. Added to that, my brother and I were also faced with the challenge of leading the church together, two pastors leading the same church. That is very uncommon in the church world today. For the most part it's not really heard of. The odds were stacked against us succeeding. Our father suddenly passed away. Our whole family was in mourning, along with the whole church.

Instead of receiving strength and support from the local pastors, some of them were making fun of us, calling our church a two-headed monster. In the midst of all this, I was working everyday at the university to support my family. As the eldest son, I began to feel the burden of responsibility of not only taking care of my wife and newborn baby. But I also felt a moral and familial obligation to help my mother, brother, and the church. The stress of all of this started to affect my health. My hair started to fall out and my body was fatigued. I soon realized I could not continue on my chosen career path and effectively fulfill my call to Pastor.

I knew I had to do something immediately. A sacrifice had to be made! All of a sudden, it came to me. I needed to quit my job. When I realized what my calling required of me, I began to gasp. I couldn't work my job and the church; it was just too much for me. But the church could not afford to bring me off my job at the time. I did receive a little stipend, but not enough to cover the cost of living. Also, I still needed to take care of my mother and brother whose sole income was through the church. This was truly my Red Sea Experience.

There is a universal law called the law of cause and effect. The basic premise behind the law is that everything happens for a reason. Successes and failures do not come by accident. You become one or the other by what you do or do not do in your life. Successful people have learned the cause-and-effect relationship between what they want and how to get it. If you want what successful people have, then you should discover what they did to get it, then do it. Don't fool yourself into thinking that you can experience success by doing what failures do. If you want to be successful, then you must *do* what successful people *do*.

Right away, I started looking at many Pastors and Bishops whom I believed were successful in their profession and whom I wanted to model my pastorate after. From that, I discovered two important truths: the first truth was that each pastor had different means and methods of becoming successful. This was enlightening because it allowed me to be able to tailor a method that was right for my brother and me to achieve success. The second truth I discovered was despite their differences, they all had one thing in common; they were all full-time Pastors. So I made the biggest decision in my life, boldly marched into my boss office and told her that I was quitting my job.

### A Ridiculous Move

Needless to say, quitting my job was not only a huge decision in my life, but one of the most ridiculous ones as well. The notion of walking off my job in hopes that church would find a way to take me on full time, plus fully support my mother and brother, was a really outlandish decision. Added to that, my job was in the midst of reorganizing the department I was in and my boss was looking to place me over another department along with the department that I was already responsible for. I was actually headed for a promotion and more money. How ridiculous, I walked away from it all.

The finances of the church were by no means stellar. Although our church is considered an influential institution in the city with a large membership, the reality was like most churches, 80 percent of them didn't support the church financially. In 1999, we had a congregation of 1500 members, with approximately 1100 of them adults, about

400 families. Out of our congregation, we were lucky to reach $380,000 in total giving for the year. This breaks down to annual gifts of $950 per family, or $345 per adult for the whole year. This may seem decent on the surface, but when you acknowledge the fact that only 20 percent actually give, we were falling way short of our potential.

We teach tithing at our church, yet only a small percentage of the people were actually doing that. For example, if we just had 20 percent of the adults in our congregation to tithe off of an assumed annual salary of $25,000, we should have been expecting at least $550,000 per year *(220 adults giving $2500)*. These same percentages are consistent in most churches, especially those that boast more than 1000 members. The more members do not necessarily mean more money, but rather much more expense and more need to train people on how to properly give to God.

As you can see, the odds of my ridiculous decision panning out weren't very hopeful. Once I announced my decision, employees, co-workers, family and friends asked the very REAL question, "Are you sure?" Some just went ahead and asked directly, "What are you going to do for money?" "Can the church afford it?" Others just simply said, "I just do not think it will work." One thing that I have discovered is that it often takes the ridiculous to produce the miraculous.

## God Gave Me A Plan

I believe it is important for you to understand I didn't just jump up and quit my job as reckless as I have made it seem. The bottom line of the matter is that I realized that in order for me to quit my job I needed to search out a method that would increase the financial giving in our church. I needed a plan. I remember hearing a preacher say, *"The plan of the Lord is the hedge of the Lord."* Knowing I needed God to keep his hedge around me, I started to research my plan by looking outside of my traditional teachings and start exploring some of the mysteries of God with regard to money and the believer.

It was during this time the criticism over prosperity preaching resurfaced. One thing I noticed right away was how the criticism seemed to stem mostly from those ministers and churches that weren't successful financially. As I continued to observe this debate, it became quite apparent to me, that it was not so much a dispute over doctrinal beliefs, nor was this just a theological disagreement, but it was more the continuance of the age old struggle between *"the haves"* and the *"have nots"* with a religious spin. After discovering this, I started to study the prosperity for myself to discover God's truth about the relationship between money and His children.

## What Happened

My discovery led me to the truth about how God desires for us to live while on earth. With this revelation, I began to teach our congregation about how to live a Kingdom lifestyle, which also deals with how we should view our relationship with money. Teaching this stuff was a gigantic risk for my brother and me, since it went against many of the traditions in the church. Looking back now, I can say that it was well worth it. Through teaching and applying these truths in my own life I have been able to live a life I believe God intends for all people to live. These truths I have named *Kingdom Keys.*

These *Kingdom Keys* have unlocked a level of independence for me spiritually and financially. They have benefited me as husband, father, son, brother, friend and pastor. These keys have also enabled me to pursue entrepreneurial opportunities that fit within my calling. Like Paul the apostle, I too can say I have all, and abound and am full. (see Philippians 4:18) Don't worry about whether this book was really written by someone who is poor trying to make a buck. God has made me rich, and is making me even richer every day.

My ultimate benefit I received from my experiences with these truths is being able to help people bridge the spiritual and economic gap in their lives, so that they can enjoy total prosperity, the way God intended for them. People who have applied these teachings have prospered tremendously and have experienced both spiritual and financial increase in their lives. The following are just some of the blessings that occurred in just the first couple of years of teaching these truths:

- Several families became debt-free
- Individuals experienced financial increase, stability and independence
- Renters turned into homeowners
- Marriages became stronger
- Entrepreneurial growth and development in membership
- Substantial increase in Tithes and Offerings
- Construction of a multimillion dollar Dr. Robert Porter Family Life Center
- Expanded community outreach where we feed and clothe over 1,000 people per month
- Established two Community Development Corporations providing after school programs, Summer Day Camps, Basketball League (more than 50 teams involved) and Indoor Soccer League
- Membership increasingly realizing their dreams and fulfilling their destinies!

These are just some of the blessings that came from these key truths about how God desires us to become wealthy for Him. It is these truths that I have written to share with you in this book.

Chapter 1

# *Why A Millionaire Mind?*

Chapter 1

# *Why A Millionaire Mind?*

*Let this mind be in you, which was also in Christ Jesus.* —Philippians 2:5

For many, becoming a millionaire represents reaching a level of financial freedom, independence and success that is found in dreams and movies. Even now in this age of billionaires such as Bill Gates, Donald Trump, Robert Johnson and Oprah Winfrey, those who have attained millionaire status in their lives are *still* both envied and respected. Yet, what is lost on so many is the potential God has given to us all to discover and develop our own inner *millionaire*!

*"But we have this* ***treasure in earthen vessels****. . ."* —2 Corinthians 4:7

There is millionaire status in everybody! God said so himself! He has placed His treasure of wealth, health and success in us His jars of clay. Now it is our job to discover it, stir it and release it!

Why *A Millionaire Mind?* Because it speaks to the treasure of greatness that lies within all of us. Greatness is not reserved to those with a particular heritage, race, or culture. Nor is it reserved just for the already rich and socially accepted. But greatness is available to those willing to believe they also can be like Christ! This is why Paul in his letter to the Church of Philippi, admonishes all believers to have the same mind as Christ had. So let's briefly consider what type of mind Christ had.

**He didn't worry about things.** Jesus didn't worry about the basic necessities of life such as food, clothes, and shelter, because He was always confident His father would provide Him with anything He asked for.

**He suffered no lack.** Christ never experienced lack in His life due to poverty; in fact, the gospels show that Jesus and His disciples had access to homes, transportation, and clothing that was considered to be luxuries during the time.

**He was sure of His calling.** Jesus knew from the very start His calling, purpose and destiny and didn't allow anything or anybody to deter him way from fulfilling it. There were many opportunities for Jesus to walk away from his purpose, but he stayed driven towards his goal. This is why we have the right to eternal life today.

**He was business minded.** The Gospels also show that Jesus was a business minded man who respected the laws of the land, paid taxes and had a treasury. In fact, Judas was entrusted to be the treasurer for the group. Jesus' business expertise attracted other men with such abilities. Peter, James and John were all entrepreneurs and Matthew was a tax collector.

**He had a great team.** The first thing that Jesus did after He came out of the desert was to start building a team. Jesus did this because He knew that one is too small a number to achieve greatness. In essence, He could not become successful by himself, so He surrounded himself with like-minded men and women who could help him accomplish his goals while he was here and to carry on the work when He left.

**He was generous.** Jesus' life displayed a lifestyle of generosity. Jesus was a giver of not only salvation, but of everyday needs. He was a healer of bodies, minds and spirits. He was kind to all people no matter their race, culture, economic or social status. He fed the hungry, encouraged the destitute, and was very generous to the poor. In fact, one of the primary reasons that the treasury existed was for the giving of alms to the poor.

**Lived a lifestyle of freedom.** Finally, Jesus' life was the perfect example of a lifestyle of freedom. He was free from fear, free from worry, free from doubt, free from traditions, and free from the opinions of men and even Satan himself, even while He was tempted. He was able to show how beneficial a lifestyle of self-discipline could be. What is even more important is He offers this same lifestyle of freedom to anyone willing to accept Him as Lord and Savior and become His disciples.

## The Myth of Money

While I am sure there are most likely many reasons for this, I believe one of the primary reasons for the church not coming into its full potential is the traditional standings and teachings regarding the relationship between God and money. For far too long leaders in the church have inappropriately used I Timothy 6:10, *"For the love of money is the root of all evil..."* in an effort of shaming the people of God to dedicate at least a portion of their money and time to the support of the church in opposed to squandering it away somewhere else. Unfortunately, this tactic has backfired on the church due to the over emphasis on sacrificial giving and the lack of it on sowing and reaping. Please understand that this is not to understate the relevance and necessity of sacrificial giving. Rather, I make this statement in order to point out the historical imbalance in the church's doctrine concerning God and money.

This doctrinal imbalance has produced a poverty mindset within the church characterized by greed, stinginess, lack, doubt, fear, anxiety and worry because of the learned belief that all God wants from us is exactly what they do not have enough of: *money*. So now congregations are filled with people who rather give God credit, instead of money. Consequently, generations and generations of people miss out on the rewards and blessings of giving and continue to live below their promise. They miss out on their inheritance and destiny only to experience a life filled with mediocrity and missed opportunities.

The Devil is a liar!!

The time has come that we stop portraying God as needy and greedy, who desires for us to give everything to Him without having the expectation of receiving. Does it not say in Luke 6:38 "when you give that it shall be given unto you?" What about Galatians 6:7 when it states, "whatever you sow, you shall reap?"

*The time has come to destroy the myth that God does not desire for His people to become wealthy.*

The time has come to destroy the myth that God does not desire for His people to become wealthy. Psalm 35:27 states that, "God finds pleasure in the prosperity of his servants." So why would it be wrong for you, as a servant of God, to desire to be prosperous if it pleases God for you to become prosperous?

Finally, it is time we stop feeling guilty about money. We need to stop feeling guilty about teaching it in the church while ignoring our need for it. Stop feeling guilty about desiring to provide ourselves and our families a better lifestyle. Stop feeling guilty for wanting to experience our dreams and achieving our goals. Stop feeling guilty for wanting to start walking in our purpose and destiny.

*Beloved, I wish above all things that thou mayest prosper and be in health, even as thy soul prospereth.* —3 John 1:2

God desires for us to be prosper in every area of our lives, including our minds, our bodies, our spirits and yes, even, in our finances. He wants every believer to experience total prosperity in their lives so they in turn could be a blessing to others.

### The Purpose of Money

One of the main reasons why people have difficulty with money is because they do not understand the *purpose* of money. When you do not understand the purpose of a thing you will abuse it. Unfortunately, I do not have to tell you that there are a lot of people abusing their money!! Just check out the increasing rate of bankruptcies, foreclosures, and repossessions occurring each year. Being impoverished and having poor credit is becoming more the rule instead of the exception these days. On the other side, you see the rich and famous being increasingly accused and convicted of fraud, embezzlement, insider trading and all sorts of white-collar crimes just to satisfy their lust for a bigger house, another luxury car, or for a fatter bank balance. Whichever category you may fit in, the truth of the matter is that all have sinned in abusing money due to our ignorance or apathy of its purpose.

So what is the purpose of money? It is to support the establishment and advancement of the Kingdom of God on the earth. One way to understand what the Kingdom of God means is by separating the word *kingdom* into two words *king* and *dom*. The word *king* refers to a person who rules as a monarch over a specific state or territory. A king is sovereign, meaning that they are self-governed and not ruled by any other state, government or persons. They have supreme authority or power over what they rule. *Dom* is short for the word *domain*. Domain is defined as the area of activity, land, or territory over which somebody has influence and control. This term deals with the ownership of a person, place or thing.

In the Bible, there are numerous accounts referring to God as King. In fact, it goes on to say that He is the "King of Kings and Lord of Lords" (Revelations 19:16). There is no one above Him. God answers to no one. He not only makes the rules, but He is the rule.

So what is His domain? The Bible says "the earth is the Lord's and the fullness thereof" (Psalms 24:1; 1Corinthians 10:26). Yet, this is not the limit to God's domain. God also rules over the heavens and the earth (see Deuteronomy 10:14). It is all His!! However, God's control became tainted with the fall of man (Adam). God had bequeathed to mankind this earth. This is why God tells Adam to have dominion over the earth (see Genesis 1:28). But Adam gave up his ownership privileges over the earth when he disobeyed God by eating of the tree. So while the earth is still the Lord's, Satan, through the acts of sinful men, controls many of the systems of this world like finance, business, and government (see Ephesians 2:2). This is why there is so much corruption found in these areas.

In Luke 19:13, Jesus tells us to *occupy* till He comes back. Occupy means to *carry on in business.* What type of business? Kingdom Business!! The establishment, increase and advancement of God's rule over the earth. Jesus' purpose on the earth was to restore man back to God. It is in this that God (king) gets back his domain (earth). God's Kingdom agenda progresses each time somebody receives salvation and becomes His disciple. Thus following the will and purpose of God in their lives. This is God's agenda for mankind. Here is the kicker, God chooses to accomplish this through us – mankind. This is the *greater work* Jesus charges us to do through the great commission:

> *Go ye therefore, and teach all nations, baptizing them in the name of the Father, and of the Son, and of the Holy Ghost: Teaching them to observe all things whatsoever I have commanded you: and, lo, I am with you alway, even unto the end of the world. Amen.* —Matthew 28:19-20

As you can see, the charge Jesus gives to us is not a small one. He expects us to reach all nations with the good news. Not just our home, neighborhoods, communities, cities or states in this country, but nations! God wants us to think and reach globally. God want us to occupy the world!! It doesn't take long to figure out this is not a cheap assignment. But in fact, it is going to take money, and lots of it to fulfill this charge. Yes, there are bills that must be paid in order to increase the Kingdom and God expects His people to take care of them!! Yet, God, in all of His wisdom made a promise to those who are willing to take care of the Kingdom.

> *And he said unto them, Verily I say unto you, There is no man that hath left house, or parents, or brethren, or wife, or children, for the kingdom of God's sake, Who shall not receive manifold more in this present time, and in the world to come life everlasting.* —Luke 18:29-30

Did you see that? God is saying for those who make the sacrifice to support His Kingdom will receive what they give up and then some, right now, in this present time. What a promise!! When you support God's Kingdom, you can expect receiving your reward today. When you replace your agenda with God's agenda God promises to prosper you! The Bible summarizes this agreement in saying,

> *But* ***seek ye first the kingdom of God****, and his righteousness;* ***and all these things shall be added unto you****.* —Matthew 6:33

I do not think it gets any clearer than that. When you seek Him first, God will program the *things* we need and desire to seek you. *You will never be last when you put God first!!* God will always honor your sacrifice with a blessing!! This is why God wants you to prosper, so He can bless you to bless the Kingdom. God is looking for distribution centers!! People who He can trust to distribute the blessings of Abraham to the earth!

## Blessed to Bless

> *And I will make of thee a great nation, and I will bless thee, and make thy name great; and* ***thou shalt be a blessing****: —Genesis 12:2*

You are blessed to bless! This is what God said to Abraham in Genesis and this is what He is saying to everybody who becomes a believer today. God's foremost reason for blessing His people is so that they will be a blessing to others through the advancement of His Kingdom! This is why God chose Abraham. God could trust Abraham enough to bless him mightily. He knew Abraham wouldn't forget about Him once he got blessed because Abraham knew the purpose for his wealth and overall prosperity. To advance God's agenda on the earth!

The truth is God wants to bless you so you can show Him off to the world. What else is a better example of the goodness of God when those who are unsaved see a saved person living the good life? What better witness is there than the world being blessed by those in the body of Christ?

The question you need to answer is, *"Can you stand to be blessed?"* Can God trust you with superstar wealth without you turning into a spoiled superstar instead of a super-servant? What is your motivation to becoming wealthy? God will not bless those who seek prosperity for prosperity sake. But God will bless those who truly desire for *God's will to be done on earth as it is in heaven (see Matthew 6:10).*

**Get Inside the Gate**

One day when I found myself depressed and questioning my purpose, the Lord spoke to my spirit and told me to look up my last name - *Porter.* Due to the state I was in I immediately questioned God because I doubted that my name was in the Bible! But the Lord kept on telling me to look it up because it held the answer I was looking for. So I went and picked up my Strong's Exhaustive Concordance of the Bible and looked up my name, Porter. Lo and behold there it was, *37 times* in the Bible. Then the Lord told me to look up what it means. So I did and found out that in the Greek language the word *porter* is transliterated as the word *shaw-ar'* meaning *gatekeeper.* Then the Lord told me to find out what they did. So I researched and found out that the gatekeepers were Levites (priests, ministers) who were responsible for guarding the city gates, the king's palace and the doors of the temple (see I Chronicles 9:17-32).

During that time, those who were outside of the city gates were the sick, lame, leprous, impoverished and destitute. Jewish law stated that the only way for them to get inside of the gate was by getting permission from the Levites to do so. No one came into the gate, until the gatekeepers invited them to come inside of the gate! This is why Jesus told the ten lepers to show themselves to the priest when they requested to be healed (see Luke 17:14). After seeing this the Lord lead me to the 100th number of Psalms where it reads:

> *Make a joyful noise unto the LORD, all ye lands. Serve the LORD with gladness: come before his presence with singing. Know ye that the LORD he is God: it is he that hath made us, and not we ourselves; we are his people, and the sheep of his pasture.* ***Enter into his gates with thanksgiving, and into his courts with praise: be thankful unto him, and bless his name.*** *For the LORD is good; his mercy is everlasting; and his truth endureth to all generations.* —Psalms 100:1-5

Right after reading the Psalm, the Lord asked me, "Do you know why they are so happy to get inside of the gate?" The answer came to me just as quickly as the question left my mind. They are happy because of what it means to be inside of the gate!! Outside of the gate is sickness, depression, disease, confusion, and desolation. But inside the gate is healing, joy, restoration, peace and prosperity!! Then the Lord said, " This is your purpose! It is in your name! I have called you to get my people inside the gate!! Never be confused again!"

God showed me my purpose through my name!! My name means gatekeeper!! In fact, I come from a line of gatekeepers! My father was a gatekeeper, and his father before him. All throughout my family, there are gatekeepers with the sole purpose to invite you, God's people, inside of the gate!! So consider this book your invitation to leave your poverty mindset and move into God's mindset!! One who knows all things are possible to them who believe!!

***There are too many Christians in the body of Christ who are not walking fully in the power of their salvation.***

*Stop living beneath your privilege and get inside the gate!*

*Stop neglecting your purpose and get inside the gate!*

*Stop letting the devil steal what's yours and get inside the gate!*

*Stop letting tradition steal you of your prosperity and get inside the gate!*

My assignment to the body of Christ is to get those from the outside to get inside of the gate. There are too many Christians in the body of Christ who are not walking fully in the power of their salvation. In this day and age of economic turmoil and uncertainty, God is looking for somebody who's willing to do whatever it takes to get inside the gate in order to advance His Kingdom. God needs people who are not burdened down with the fear and guilt of becoming rich so He may bless them to be rich in someone else's life. He needs someone who is not so impressed with money to the point that they that they fall in love with it. Instead, God needs somebody who knows the purpose of money. God needs a servant who can handle a superstar blessing and live in the increase so the Word of the Lord will be preached to all of creation!!

In essence, He is looking for somebody with *a Millionaire Mind.*

Are you the one?

Chapter 2

# *Kingdom Keys*

## Chapter 2

# *Kingdom Keys*

*The heart of the prudent acquires knowledge, And the ear of the wise seeks knowledge.*
—Proverbs 18:15

Contrary to popular opinion, the number one form of wealth is not money, but knowledge!! Knowledge is the key to unlocking unlimited wealth and success in your life. The difference between those who *"have"* and those who *"have not"* is what they know and the application of it in their lives. In order to realize your God given potential for becoming prosperous, you have to have an unquenchable thirst for learning about God's system for your success. It is all about seeking the knowledge of God.

How would you like to be able to achieve every goal, attain every dream, and receive everything the Lord has for you? Wouldn't it be wonderful to not have to worry if you will have enough money at the end of the month? Wouldn't you love to be able to not only afford what you need, but afford to get all of your wants? How about sending your children to the best schools? Have a wonderful marriage? Be able to be a generous giver and receiver? Well, according to Jesus, all of these things and more are available to those who take time to learn of Him and his ways.

Jesus said once we seek the Kingdom of God in our lives, then every *thing* shall be given to us (see Matthew 6:33). You may ask what He means by "things". I believe what Jesus meant was referring to not only the necessities of life (food, clothes, shelter, and transportation), but also the luxuries of life that raise the quality of how you live. Unfortunately, too many people have ended up without both necessities and luxuries because of their ignorance of the process of how to get them. Consequently, they end up stuck chasing after things instead of things chasing after them. They are unable to unlock the door to these things God has placed on the earth to improve their lives and enable them to fulfill their destiny because they do not possess *keys* to them.

## The Kingdom of God

Many times when the *Kingdom of God or the Kingdom of Heaven* is used in scripture, it is commonly considered to refer to the physical paradise Christians go to after they pass on from this earth to heaven. Though correct to one extent, this belief does not fully capture the entire truth of the meaning represented from these phrases. The Kingdom of God or Heaven is not limited to a place, but are used to describe a whole other reality based on the sovereign will of God.

The Kingdom of God is a system. It is God's way of doing and being right. So when Jesus said to seek ye first the Kingdom of God (heaven), He was stating we should seek first God's way or system of doing and being right in our lives. Once you do this in every area of your life, you are showing God and the world you are willing to live a life that is submitted to God's rule. That you've accepted God's agenda over your own. It is through this type of lifestyle that allows you access to God's blessings and favor. In essence, if you are to attain *a Millionaire Mind* then you must first possess a Kingdom Consciousness.

## Principles - Keys to Kingdom Living

The only way to be successful at adopting God's agenda in your life is by understanding and applying the principles of God in your life. I like to call them *Kingdom Keys,* because it is through them that you gain access to the abundant life Jesus promised in John 10:10. I don't know about you, but I desire more for my life and the lives of my family and those I pastor. In fact, I desire more for you, that is the reason for this book. **Life submitted to the rule of God is the key to experiencing more.**

Let me reiterate, *Kingdom Keys* are synonymous to principles. I have named them *Kingdom Keys* because principles are the keys to *Kingdom Living.* You cannot live a life under God's rule if you do not possess knowledge of them. One of the major problems in many churches is the lack of knowledge of God's principles. Due to their ignorance we now see the realization of this prophecy by Hosea.

*My people are destroyed for **lack of knowledge**....* —Hosea 4:6a

What is the knowledge Hosea is talking about? It is the principles of God. His way of doing and being right. God's principles cannot be overlooked or marginalized. If you do not know His principles you will suffer the consequences. Hosea goes on to say that if you forget God's law it will cause God to forget you. Why? Because you are not acting like His children. So although you may be saved and going to heaven, you will miss out on God's favor and blessings on earth. This is how many who are saved, who say that they love the Lord, experience no change in their earthly circumstances even though they possess eternal life.

*God's principles cannot be overlooked or marginalized.*

Due to their ignorance or indifference to God's principles, there is the tendency for most people to over spiritualize and super-naturalize the blessings of God that are in reality simply the products of an ancient system fashioned by God. What makes this tendency so dangerous to the Christian is the belief that God must move supernaturally in order for the believer to be blessed. Hence, the believer only experiences blessings sporadically at best believing, somehow, God only wishes to bless them only at certain times during the course of their lives. They are totally ignoring the truth that the reason why they are not experiencing blessings at a consistent rate is because they are not taking advantage of the principles of God in their lives.

## Principles Defined

Principles are simple yet powerful models that help us understand how the world works according to God. They are synonymous to laws, which generate the same results each and every time. You do not have to believe in a principle for it to work. They will work regardless of what you believe. For example consider the principle or law of gravity. I do not care how much you believe it won't work, if you do not respect it or apply it, and decided to run off a two story building, you will still fall to the earth and injure yourself.

Principles not only work whether you believe in them or not, but like keys they will work for anybody who uses them. That's right. Anybody! You do not even have to be saved to be able to benefit from them. They will work just as good for a sinner as it will for a saint. Principles are like keys to a brand new Bentley. The keys will unlock the doors and start its engine no matter who uses it.

## Access to Heaven's Power

Probably the most significant aspect of principles or *Kingdom Keys* is their accessibility to heaven's power. When you live your life under the rule of God, you gain access to spiritual power that is promised to Jesus' called out ones. That is the spiritual authority of binding and loosing.

> *"And I also say to you that you are Peter, and on this rock I will build My church, and the gates of Hades shall not prevail against it. "And I will give you the keys of the kingdom of heaven, and whatever you bind on earth will be bound in heaven, and whatever you loose on earth will be loosed in heaven."*—Matthew 16:18-19 (NKJV)

Many people have mistakenly limited the power of binding and loosing to that of casting out demons, calling forth healing or even financial gain. However, God has given you and I so much more through this gift of binding and loosing.

What I have learned is true binding and loosing is not just based solely on what you say, but rather works in conjunction with how you live. You can say what you will, but it will be ineffective if you do not live it. If you bind sickness and loose healing into your body, then you must walk in what you say by faith until it manifests in your life. Most people are not experiencing the results of what they say because they do not believe enough in it to walk in it. You must believe it to walk in it, and you must walk in it in order to receive it.

How do you walk until you receive? By living your life according to the principles of God. Only once you do this will you be able to get heaven to work with you on your situation. If you want to move heaven on your behalf you must walk by faith and not by sight. Then and only then will you gain access to spiritual power in heaven that will echo your actions on earth.

### There's A Key to Every Gate

Understanding that your lifestyle gains you access to heaven's power is critical to your success in pursuit of an abundant life. Why? Because each *Kingdom Key* will give you the heavenly power needed to unlock each gate that the Devil tries to place in your life.

> *"And I also say to you that you are Peter, and on this rock I will build My church, and **the gates of Hades** shall not prevail against it. **And I will give you the keys of the kingdom of heaven**."* —Matthew 16:18

Another term that can be used to describe the gates Satan uses to try to thwart our blessings is *strongholds.*

> *For the weapons of our warfare are not carnal but mighty in God for pulling down **strongholds**, casting down arguments and every high thing that exalts itself against the knowledge of God, bringing every thought into captivity to the obedience of Christ.* —2 Corinthians 10:4-5 (NKJV)

Strongholds are those thoughts Satan places in our minds that hinder us from realizing the promises of God for our lives. Satan uses negative thoughts as gates keep us away from our blessings promised by God. There are many gates he uses to keep us away from experiencing extraordinary wealth, peace of mind, fabulous relationships, true love, overwhelming happiness and spiritual authority. Although this sounds bad, we must realize for every gate God has given a key. In fact, it is not a regular key but a *Kingdom Key* with *Kingdom Power*. This means for every hellish problem there is a heavenly solution. That's right! God has a solution for every problem the devil throws your way. Truly no weapon formed will prosper, once you surrender to the rule of God in your life.

In this book, I will be sharing with you certain *Kingdom Keys* I have discovered in my life, which have given me heavenly access to more than I could ever imagine or think (see Ephesians 3:20). They are keys that have enabled me to not only survive tragedy and loss, but have enabled me to discover my destiny and pursue my purpose with passion. Due to my discovery of these keys, I have a life full of favor and privilege with more on the way. Not only am I excited about my future, but I am excited about my today and you will be too once you learn and apply these *Kingdom Keys* to your life.

Always remember, God is not a respecter of people, but is a respecter of principles. Once you discover this, you too can unlock the millionaire in you. So turn the page to start receiving the *Kingdom Keys* that will unlock the gates blocking the abundance and favor into your life!

Chapter 3

Kingdom Key #1

# *It All Starts In Your Mind*

## Chapter 3

### Kingdom Key #1

# *It All Starts In Your Mind*

*As a man thinks in his heart, so is he....* —Proverbs 23:7a

You are the fruit of your thoughts. The very way you act, talk, walk, dress, eat and live is determined by thoughts that were sown and nourished in the soil of your mind throughout the duration of your lifetime. Thoughts determine your habits, behavior and character. The very reason why you are where you are in your life is because of your current mindset. If you have a mindset of poverty and lack, then your life is one of poverty and lack. But if you have a mindset of abundance and opportunity, then your life will be filled with abundance and opportunity. Proverbs 23:7 says it best, *"as a man thinkest in his heart, so is he"*.

What are you thinking?

### The Pursuit To Be Average

In the book *Focal Point,* author and motivational speaker, Brian Tracy states, "We are now living in the most prosperous age in human history. More people are achieving financial independence and becoming millionaires today, at a faster rate than ever before." [1] So the question is, "Why aren't you one of these people?" The answer to this question is simply because you have not put your mind to it.

Most of us have been programmed to live a life of mediocrity at best and failure at worst. From well meaning family members, to teachers, preachers and civic leaders, most (if not all) have encouraged us how to get good grades, go to college, get a good paying job, get married and have children, put them through college, retire and spoil the grandchildren, and go to heaven. Not to knock this advice, I believe we should do all of these things as well. But isn't everyone encouraged to do this? If everyone is encouraged to achieve it, then wouldn't it make this the standard or average thing to do?

*Most of us have been programmed to live a life of mediocrity at best and failure at worst.*

Now ask yourself, when have you been encouraged to not be average, to not be like everybody else. Not in a negative way, but in a positive one? For many of you, it was when you were a child. Remember, you were asked what you would like to become when you grew up and you would say a fireman, policeman, or the President of the United States. Then they would say go for it, you can do it.

What happened?

Some of you may say, life happened, and reality set in. So you decided to become like everyone else, ordinary, average and mediocre. There are some who are reading this book who were like me, very successful at being average. In fact, you have excelled in your pursuit of becoming average. You have the degrees, the marriage, the kids, the house in the suburbs, the social status, and a good job, and you feel like you're pretty much on track with your life.

Then there are some of you who might be struggling just to be average. You are divorced, single with kids, not in a great relationship, not much formal education, working a job you hate, and it always seems like you have more month than money all the time.

Then there are some who are reading this that may say you are down right failing at being average. You are struggling to survive. It seems everywhere you turn you are faced with trouble!! Trouble in your home, trouble on your job (when you have one), trouble in your finances, trouble in your mind, even trouble with your health. Your life is filled with just plain old trouble, trouble, trouble.

Whatever condition you are in, I believe deep down inside of you there is a desire and potential to be *more*. You want to be more than average, be more than ordinary, be more than mediocre, and be more than what you are right now.

Guess what? You can be more!!

### A Destiny Decision

Experiencing more starts with the decision to be more than what you are right now. Many people gave up on their dreams a long time ago and simply never brought it back to their memory. Others decided to settle for wishing and hoping, than deciding on doing something about their situation. Well, it is time to reprogram your mind. You need to make one of the most important decisions of your life. A destiny decision. Decide NOW that you will be more than average, more than ordinary and have more than enough. Remember as a man thinks so is he. You can start to realize your dreams and tap into the wealth that is inside of you by simply making this decision to change your mind.

*Change your mind from being ordinary to extraordinary!*

*Change your mind from being average to being great!*

*Change your mind from settling to asking for what you want!*

*Becoming more starts with the decision to be more!*

In order for you to make this move, you need to start thinking outside the status quo. You cannot think like everybody else. You cannot look at your situation like everybody else does. You must look at your life from the eye of possibilities than limitations! In Philippians, Paul said, "I can do all things through Jesus Christ who strengthens me" (Philippians 4:13). This is coming from a man who spent nearly all of his life in prison. Yet, he still declared that he could do it all!!

You need to know no matter what your situation is right now, you can do it all!! Why, because you have Jesus Christ, the son of the living God as your partner. All things are possible through him. All you need to do is to start making your mind like Christ's—*A Millionaire Mind.*

### The Power to Manifest

When you start thinking about how you want your life to be, what type of relationships you want to have, what you want to do in your life, how much you want to earn, and what you want to accomplish in your life, you will start to suddenly see *miracles* manifest in your life. Your life will turn from experiencing blessings here and there to a life of favor.

*Everything you see began as a thought in someone's mind.*

Once I made the decision to stop pursuing being average and to start pursuing being more in my mind, I suddenly became aware of the many opportunities available of reaching my dreams and goals I couldn't see before. It was like a dam was lifted in my brain. Plans, strategies and ideas seemed to flood my mind on how I could accomplish the goals I had set for myself. My thoughts started to become things in my life. Actual ideas and concepts, turned into tangible things that allowed me to walk off my job and experience the freedom that I have right now. How? Through the power of manifestation.

Look around you. Everything you see began as a thought in someone's mind. The chair you are sitting on. The book you are reading. The clothes you are wearing and even the food that you may be snacking on right at this minute. All were first a thought, then, a thing brought forth out of nothing.

The verb for turning thoughts into things is "to manifest." It comes from the Middle English word *Manifestus,* meaning *visible* and the Latin word *manus* meaning *hand.* According to the authors of the *One Minute Millionaire,* Mark Victor Hansen and Robert Allen, when you manifest something you,

"Metaphorically reach your hand through the invisible curtain separating the tangible world from the world of imagination and pull your desired object into existence. First, you think it and then, you manifest it. You materialize it. You cause it to appear."[2]

**You Are What You Think**

I am sure you have heard the cliché, "You are what you eat." Well, here is a new one, "*you are what you think.*" The power to manifest, to turn thoughts into things, is not restricted to just certain people. The truth is everyone has this God given ability. Everyone has the power to manifest! It all starts in the mind. This is why we see the apostle Paul encouraging the Christians in Rome and to believers everywhere the following,

> *And be not conformed to this world: but be ye transformed by the renewing of your mind, that ye may prove what is that good, and acceptable, and perfect, will of God.*
> —Romans 12:2

The best thing I can do for you is to help you change your thinking!! If I can encourage you to change your thinking, then you will start to change your life. This is why God's first request to Abraham was to leave his country so God could get him away from a place that promoted his old mindset. Drastic as it sounds, you may need to leave your "country" as well. This may mean leaving friends, family, or even your church that doesn't teach about God's desire for you to prosper and pursue your dreams. No matter what, change your thinking at any means necessary. Your future depends upon it.

The reason why I list this as the first *Kingdom Key* is because if you do not realize it all *starts in your mind* then the rest of this book will not help you at all. Every thought has consequences. No thought resides in your brain rent-free. *You are what you think.* If you allow thoughts filled with negativity and lack rule your mind, then you are guaranteeing a life filled with poverty and pessimism. If you think your life cannot turn around and things cannot get better, then your life will *never* turn around and *never* get better.

## The Key to Changing Your Mind

So you now accept and acknowledge your need to change your thinking, but you do not know how or where to start. So let's look at what the word says about how to renew your mind.

> *This book of the law shall not depart out of thy mouth; but thou shalt meditate therein day and night, that thou mayest observe to do according to all that is written therein: for then thou shalt make thy way prosperous, and then thou shalt have good success.*
> —Joshua 1:8

God told Joshua if he would meditate upon the law (God's Word) day and night, observe it then it would make his way prosperous and successful. So the answer to the question of how to accomplish the renewing of our minds is meditating upon God's Word. If you are honest with yourself, you know you do not spend enough time studying God's Word. Unfortunately, you are not alone in this. Just check out any Wednesday night Bible study, where there are always more pews than people in attendance. I state this not to make you feel guilty, but to help you realize where you can start this process. Just go to Bible study.

Meditation involves three fundamentals in order to produce the results expected. They are *words, images and emotions*. Through meditation these three elements are used to create a picture or vision in your mind of the goal in which you want to achieve or accomplish. God used this concept many times in the Bible with his prophets. He communicated to them through a vision or a dream in order to tell them what he wanted them to know and do. This is the same concept advertisers use when doing a commercial. They use words to communicate the message they want usually via a jingle (a catchy tune). Then they produce an image or in this case images of the product, to show what it does and how effective it is. Then they make sure they use a spokesperson or situation that will establish a connection with us and provides a certain level of trustworthiness. Then they constantly repeat it with the intent to get into our subconscious mind. So when we go to the store, we will pass up a product with the same ingredients that is cheaper because the manufactures did not pay for marketing. We go ahead and buy the brand name product at a higher cost because of the commercial.

What am I saying? We meditate everyday without knowing it! We are constantly bombarded with commercials using words, images and emotions from life circumstances, our environments, society, the news, and radio, all shaping what and how we think and, eventually, act. However, what God is saying is He wants us to form a commercial of His Word, in our minds. Through constant meditation of God's Word you will start to see yourself as God sees you. When you start to see yourself in this light, you start to behave differently. Your attitude changes. You are no longer the same depressed and stressed-out person because you have a better self-image of yourself. You are more confident because of the confidence in God's Word.

After your attitude changes, then your actions change. You start to respond rather than react to challenges. Instead of allowing your emotions to rule you, you rule your emotions. Now you feel free to obey God's Word because you see, in your mind, the goal in which God has set for you to achieve. Your destiny is clear and your future is bright. So the fear of going after it is overcome with expectation of achieving it!! Once you start to walk in obedience to God's will for your way, your success is automatic. Just look at what Job said.

> *If they obey and serve him, they shall spend their days in prosperity, and their years in pleasures.* —Job 36:11

Your success and prosperity is available to you *now*!! But you won't be able to realize it until you *see* it!!

*You have to see yourself healthy in order to be healed!*

*You have to see yourself happy in order to have a joy!*

*You have to see yourself triumphant in order for you to have victory!*

In order to accomplish this, you must have a solid foundation of truth you base your identity on. There is no better foundation to do this with than the Holy Word of God. The very Word from the One who created us. The Bible is the how-to manual of His handiwork. So why not use it?

The main reason so many are living under their privilege and not realizing their millionaire potential is because they base themselves on the things of this world. According to these things, one moment you are great and accepted while in the next you are considered a freak and an outcast. No wonder there are so many confused people walking around today. Our only hope and refuge lies in the truth of God's Word. For it is He that has created us and not we ourselves, we are the sheep of His pasture (see Psalms 100). So why not set your mind on the Word so you can manifest what God says, instead of what the world says!!

No matter what your situation is right now. You can start again today. Take back your mind and submit it to the will of God. Transform and renew your mind by meditating upon God's Word. Start to see yourself as God sees you. Define yourself off of his truth instead of the lies of this world. This is your first step towards discovering your inner-millionaire.

Thoughts turn into things. Some people manifest abundance. Others manifest lack. If you do not have what you want, examine your thoughts. Remember it all starts in the mind. So what type of mind do you have?

Choose right now to have *a Millionaire Mind!*

Chapter 4

Kingdom Key #2

# *You Are Your Wealth*

## Chapter 4

### Kingdom Key #2

# *You Are Your Wealth*

*And you shall remember the Lord your God, for it is He who gives you power to get wealth....* —Deuteronomy 8:18a

Everything you need to manifest wealth lies inside of you. Yet, so many go though life never tapping into their wealth potential because they belief their source of wealth is external than internal. This is why it is so important to renew your mind with God's Word so that you may be able to see the absolute truth that *you are your wealth!* One of the keys to realizing this is by truly understanding your worth.

### You Are Valuable

Do you know how valuable you are? If not, think about this. Out of the six billion people on the planet, there is only *one* you. You are so unique in design that nobody else has your same fingerprints, palm prints, or footprints. Even the rhythm of your heartbeat is exclusive only to you. This tells me that you and I weren't massed produced, but custom-made. In the fashion industry, clothes that are custom-made are more expensive because they are made-to-order. Similarly, your value is so high because of your distinctive design is made-to-order for this particular time you live in. You are precious, matchless, and one-of-a-kind. Once you pass from this reality, no one else or thing can replace you. You know what that makes you? Priceless!!

The reason why it is so critical to understand your worth is so you can start realizing the awesome amount of potential you actually possess. The Bible tells us we were created in God's image (see Genesis 1:26). To fully understand what this means, one must start to understand aspects of God's character.

One important facet of God's nature essential to learn is found in the account of the creation. In it we are shown when God created the heavens and the earth, He did so from within Himself. Once He spoke "Let there be" it was immediately so without any external assistance. In fact all living things, were created solely from the will of God.

Since we are fashioned in God's image, we too possess this same quality, the power of creation. We are co-creators with God! We too have the ability to call things that are not, and bring them into existence. Like God we do not need to depend upon the external to produce our needs and desires because of the vast resources that God instilled in each one of us. Unfortunately, too many of us have accepted the lie that we are unable to control this aspect of our lives. Yet, nothing can be further from the truth. All we have to do to manifest wealth is by tapping into our very own God given creative power.

## Discovering and Developing your Gifts

The way we tap into our creative power is through the discovery and development of the unique talents, skills and abilities God has planted inside each one of us. The Bible refers to these attributes as *gifts*. I believe the Bible calls them gifts because it alludes to the treasure that lies hidden within us. One of the simple reasons why people do not represent their inner worth is because they simply refuse to open the gifts God has given to them. Therefore, never getting a chance to realize the potential benefits of what lies inside.

Solomon tells us *"a man's gift makes room for him, and brings him before great men."* (Proverbs 18:16) In other words, the key to realizing our inner wealth lies in our gifts. Gifts lead to treasure. Once we develop and exercise our gifts, then we can create opportunities or *rooms* for wealth to come into our lives. The converse of the scripture is also true. Where there is no gift, there is no treasure. Thus, gifts that go undeveloped do not create rooms or opportunities for wealth.

Again, many fail to tap into their inner wealth because they are not committed to the development of their gifts. However, there are some who fail to do so because they do not believe they possess any gifts at all. They feel they aren't gifted because their gifts aren't expressed as others are around them. They cannot sing or play an instrument or are not as talented or smart as other people seem to be. Consequently, they get caught in the trap of being so envious and jealous of somebody else's gifts that they are blind to the unique attributes God has given to them. Blind to what sets them apart from everyone else.

Just because you do not have the same talents and skills as somebody else does not mean God skipped you on the day He was passing out gifts. Just like we all have a measure of faith, God has given each of us our own unique measure of gifts. God did so because He wants us to learn it is our differences that determine our value. I am sure anyone who has walked into a place and saw someone with the same outfit as you, know what I mean. You are immediately disappointed because you have discovered your outfit wasn't as unique as you thought and therefore it lost some of its value in your eyes. Why? Because it is the differences in a thing, place or person that determines its' value. So the first action required of us to begin to tap into our inner wealth is to discover and accept our own unique gifts.

Discovering what your gifts are is relatively simple. For the most part it is those things you are naturally good at doing. For some their gifts are artistic such as painting, singing, playing an instrument, or in the performance arts. For others, it is having an aptitude for arithmetic, languages, economics, or business. Then there are those who are good at organizing, managing, and leading people. There are, of course many, many more areas of aptitude that can be listed. However, the point is every one of us are good at doing something, and whatever that is, it is, more than likely, one of our gifts.

Discovering what your gifts are alone will not automatically create for you opportunity. Gifts must be developed in order to get the best results from out of them. A lot of people tend to take their gifts for granted and think just because they are talented or smart in an area they are due certain results or rewards. But this isn't true at all. Remember, everybody possesses a gift, so having a gift is not what makes you standout in the crowd. What does however, is developing your gift to the point that you can optimally utilize it any given moment.

For example, I always run into a lot of people who possess the talent to sing or play an instrument who are looking to break into the gospel music industry. Unfortunately, it is not these people who usually make it because they do not understand that it takes more than just talent to develop a music career. Just because you are the best singer or musician in your church, school, or family, doesn't mean you are automatically have what it takes to go to the next level. What it does take however, is someone who is willing to faithfully develop their gift through consistent practice and by learning the profession they plan to apply it in.

Too many people have a welfare mentality believing the only way for them to achieve their dreams is by looking to others to give them a hand up, a hand out, or their big break. While I do believe that true success cannot be achieved without the help of others, relying solely upon somebody else for your success is setting yourself up for failure and a whole lot of heartbreak. You must value yourself highly enough to realize the state of your future is ultimately up to how you use what God gave you. Which means you must make the investment of developing you gift. The more developed your gift becomes, the more rooms or opportunities will become available to you. Also a mature gift will attract the type of people you need to make your dreams a reality.

A truth I learned early on in life is ***people like to help those who help themselves.*** This truth is so powerful it could easily qualify as a *Kingdom Key* itself. One thing you need to realize in your life is that people are busy and do not automatically owe you their attention or assistance. It is not until you show proof of how badly you want your dreams that you will gain the help you need. Remember it is your gift, so you need to do everything possible to develop it. Your gift will be able to place you before great men who can help you reach your dreams. In essence, what you need to develop is: You, Incorporated.

## You, Incorporated

You are worth the investment. The investment of your time, your attention and all your resources to develop the most important resource in your life: *you*. You must look at yourself as the CEO of You, Incorporated. As CEO, your primary responsibility is to manage yourself in a manner that will maximize your potential enough to guarantee success in your life.

Like a corporation, You, Incorporated are made up of assets and liabilities otherwise known as strengths and weaknesses. It is critical that you take the time to identify which traits are your assets and liabilities. Write them down by categorizing them. For example, you may be very creative, but lack organizational skills. So under the strengths or assets category creativity should be listed. Similarly, organization should be listed under weaknesses or liabilities (see Diagram 1). Once a business identifies their assets and liabilities, they then seek methods on how to further develop their strengths and diminish their liabilities.

| Assets (Strengths) | Liabilities (Weaknesses) |
|---|---|
| Creativity | Organization |
| Personable | Analytical |
| Communicative | Follow Through |

*Diagram 1*

This is the same process you want to apply in your life, develop your strengths and diminish your weaknesses. Most people make the mistake of doing the exact opposite by trying to improve their weaknesses and virtually ignore their strengths, which ultimately diminishes them. The reason why this strategy is flawed is because no matter what you do or how much time you spend trying to improve your weaknesses; they will never become a strength in your life. You will always be weak in that area. So how do you improve your overall productivity? By focusing on developing your strengths. Think about it. What makes you stand out from the crowd? What is it that distinguishes you from the other six billion people on the planet? Your strengths! Those things you and only you are awesome at doing! You do not want to ignore them while trying to improve on a weakness that will become average at best. It is your strengths, and them alone, that will guarantee the success of You, Inc.

## The Importance of Education

Assessment of your strengths and weaknesses is only the start of maximizing your potential. The next step in this process is to take advantage of the tools and opportunities that will optimize your inner resources. One tool that is critical for you to take advantage of is education.

*A common characteristic successful businesses share is their priority on education.*

A common characteristic successful businesses share is their priority on education. It is a priority because innovation is often times the offspring of education. It is through these new ideas, concepts and processes that usually give a corporation the competitive edge in their industry. This also holds true for your personal corporation, You, Inc. If you are to become competitive in your life and realize your potential, then you must invest in your education.

Making the decision to make education a priority will only add value to You, Inc. It levels out the playing field of life and enables you to at least be competitive in not only your vocation, but also life in general. Being talented or gifted is not enough. You must know how to effectively optimize your gifts so that they will manifest into what you ultimately desire. How many times have you heard the horror stories of talented individuals athletically or musically who had the skills, but didn't have the knowledge to protect their gifts from becoming abused? Too many!! Why? Because they didn't have the schooling needed to recognize a bad deal and possess the sense that they would be better off to hire professional help so that they wouldn't get ripped-off.

Athletes and musicians aren't the only ones this occurs to. Everyday people from every walk of life are judged, treated and labeled in part by how educated they are. Those you come in contact with everyday are interviewing you. They are judging you by your looks, conversation and mannerism. If you look, sound or act a certain way, then you will ultimately be treated that way. No matter what the facts are. It isn't fair, but it is the reality we live in. This is how potential geniuses are regulated to average jobs, or no jobs at all, because they didn't understand how crucial education was to making a good first impression.

## Education and Poverty

If knowing you are judged everyday by what you know is not motivation enough to invest in your education, then what about knowing that it is a crucial determinant of those who "have" and those who "have not". It has been proven there is a direct link between minimal educational attainment and high poverty rates. Basically, a person with minimum education is likely to attain employment at a low paying job. Employment at a low paying job leads to the likelihood of subsistence living, better known as welfare. Living on welfare usually leads to a life of poverty that is ultimately passed down from generations to generations.

As immoral as racism and discrimination is in America, there is a greater threat to those who are labeled "minorities" in our country. This threat is poverty. It just so happens that minorities make up more in this category because of our country's racist history. America faced this ugly truth with the destruction caused by Hurricane Katrina in New Orleans, Louisiana. Although the actual hurricane didn't cause much damage to the city, breaks in the levees, caused by the storm, occurred allowing the Northern Gulf to flood into what was once called Crescent City. The result was eighty percent of New Orleans underwater. There was a call for residents to evacuate the city because of the force of the hurricane and many did evacuate in time. Yet, sadly, many did not.

The destruction of the storm was horrific. Everything from casinos to churches, hotels to whole neighborhoods were totally destroyed, but that wasn't the worst of it. That arrived when those who could not get out of the city before the storm were herded to the Superdome and Convention Center in Downtown New Orleans with no food, no water and no plan on how to get them to safety. They were mostly African American, some were elderly and disabled, but the majority was poor.

The government's reaction was extremely slow. Assistance didn't come for days allowing chaos and mayhem to breakout among those who survived. Horror stories of suicides, rapes and murder among unlivable conditions were prevalent in the news. Ironically, the news media could make it in the city while the government could not. Consequently, many more died than there should have because of our government's slow response. This immediately raised the question of why help did not get there earlier. Many pointed to the issue of race, which the government vehemently denied. But the sad truth is the issue of race was actually secondary to the reality of the devastating number of people who were living impoverished prior to the storm.

2000 census data reported that more than one in four, 28 percent, of the city's residents were living in poverty before the hurricane descended upon the city. Of the 245 large cities in the nation with populations of 100,000 or more, New Orleans tied for the sixth poorest in the 2000 census.[1] Because of this reality, many could not respond to the warnings to evacuate the city because they lacked the transportation or money to do so. ***They could not afford to save their own lives.*** Consequently, many people died, suffered and lost everything. Their lives were devastated because they lacked the knowledge and means to do so.

The lesson that needs to be learned from this tragedy is that it doesn't pay to be poor in America or anywhere else. Unfortunately, many choose to do so because they write off education. No it is not the only solution to challenging Bill Gates position as the wealthiest man in the world, but as you can see, it is one choice that could enable you to save your own life.

Hopefully, through this real world example, you can see there is a price you pay when you avoid developing what you have inside. Can you not see that you are worth the little time, effort and expense of becoming the best you can be? I also hope you are able to identify and defeat any barrier that attempts to prohibit you from discovering and developing your inner wealth.

## Low Self-Worth

One of the most prevailing diseases in the world is depression. The World Health Organization says depression rate is doubling every ten years and will be, by 2020, the most pervasive illness in the world (currently second only to heart disease) and the second major cause of death. One of the leading causes of depression is low self-worth, which consists of feelings of inadequacy and inferiority. People who suffer from this tend to believe they do not have what it takes to be successful, and anything they do will result in failure. For this cause, many do not even attempt to improve their social and/or economic status in life because of the certainty in their mind that it will not work.

One would think this condition is not as prevalent among Christians, but sadly this isn't true. Churches across America are filled with people who suffer from some form of depression because of low self-worth. It is this very issue that is one of the most predominant barriers for many to discovering their inner wealth.

Low self-worth is common in America because of the constant pressure to meet society's standards of what it means to be smart, beautiful, rich and successful. The pressure is so intense most people spend their lives trying to reach them by emulating celebrities and sports figures, flaws and all, to gain a sense of value. They figure if they could be like Michael Jordan, Oprah

Winfrey, Bill Gates, or even T.D. Jakes, they would automatically have what these celebrities have. Consequently, people lose their own identities and miss out on discovering their inner greatness trying to become what they are not.

As much as I admire certain famous personalities and believe there are a lot of benefits to learn from their life experiences, it is not worth sacrificing my potential in order to be like someone else. There is an inherent flaw in trying to be somebody else. That person already exists. So no matter what you do and how much time and money you invest to imitate someone, the sad fact is you will never ever *be* them. All you will be known as is a cheap copy. I don't know about you, but I believe God did not intend to make us as copies of one another, but as distinctive originals. So it is our duty, as God's creations, to not aspire to be cheap copies of one another, but great originals of ourselves.

## Risk of Failure

Another issue used as a barrier to discovering our inner wealth is the risk of failure. I do not know of anyone who actually enjoys failing. I, also, do not know of anyone who has not failed. The bottom line is ultimately each of us will make a mistake that causes us to fall short of our goals some time or another. In short, we will fail. Yet, even though failure is inevitable in our lives, it does not lessen its emotional, psychological and sometimes physical impact. Many times failure not only affects just one person, but also those associated with the one who has failed.

Like the struggling parents who find themselves single after failing in their marriage, not only do they have to live with the consequences resulting from a bad marriage, but now, their children must deal with them as well. Consequently, it is very possible their failure can turn into a curse that passes from generation to generation. They may find themselves struggling in creating and maintaining significant relationships in their lives. Due to such results, most will do anything to avoid the risk of failing all together and decide to do all they can to play it safe. They will settle for an average life, achieving average things with average people. Unaware of doing so, they actually lessen their chances of ever achieving anything spectacular at all.

If you are to ever experience true success in life you must first risk failing. This is so because of the crisis that it creates. While many look at experiencing crisis as a bad thing, it really should be considered good, because it pushes us out of our current comfort zone. In essence, it requires change. Unfortunately, change does not come easy to most of us because we are creatures of comfort. It often takes a traumatic or violent event to shake us up enough to make us want to modify our habits to do something new. In fact, for most, if it wasn't for them failing, they would be worse off than what they are now. I know many people who had to almost die in order for them to be alive right now. Sadly, they had to almost experience the ultimate failure in order to make the change.

*If you are to ever experience true success in life you must first risk failing.*

**Don't Let Your Faith Fail**

One of the primary reasons why people fear failing is because they do not understand its true purpose. Contrary to popular opinion, failure is not supposed to destroy you, nor is it to prevent you from achieving your goals. Rather, the true intent of failure is to help develop and mature you on your path to success. Due to this, failure is an essential component in the system of success.

As you can see, failure is all about perspective. The reason why people fear the risk of failing is because of how they've perceived it to be a destroying agent in their lives. But God never meant for your failure to destroy you, nor does God judge you for your failure. *That statement alone is worth the price of this book!* God does not judge our failure! So why are you so down on yourself and feeling so guilty about failing? It is a part of life and God understands this. He even said it in His Word.

> *And the Lord said, Simon, Simon, behold, Satan hath desired to have you, that he may sift you as wheat: But I have prayed for thee, that thy faith fail not.* —Luke 22:31-32

Isn't this refreshing? Jesus is telling us "Simons" He knows life is not easy. In fact, most of the time it is a struggle because Satan is always after us seeking to sift us like wheat. So it is crazy to think we won't mess up and make the wrong decisions from time to time. But Jesus is telling us to not panic when we do fail. Instead, He let's us know He is always praying for us, so that, in our failure, we do not let our faith fail!

You see life is and will never be about playing it safe. Instead, life is designed for risk-takers who are not afraid to live it on the edge. If you are ever going to experience all the fullness and wonder life has to offer, you must be willing to stretch yourself almost to the point of breaking in order to get it. How is this accomplished? By faith!! If you are to make it in this life, you must live it at risk, on the edge, in faith. For the Bible tells us, *"the just shall live by faith!"* (Hebrew 10:38)

This means you are going to have to endure a whole lot of "no's" before you get to your "yes". People will tell you, "no" to your dreams, "no" to your choices, and "no" to your ideas. You will be criticized, ridiculed, embarrassed, and humiliated. People you once thought were with you until the end will turn their backs on you right when you need them the most. You will experience all of the pain and sorrow failure brings. But if you hold on to your passion, hold on to your dream, and mostly hold on to your faith you will receive what faith rewards!

Are you now seeing why you cannot afford to play it safe and risk not failing? Failure leads to faith and there is nothing more pleasing to God than those who live life by faith!! Faith rewards faith! It is a promise from God Himself. True success only comes from the pursuit of goals that are beyond your reach! Your dreams and goals are supposed to be too big, too ambitious, and too expensive because that's what activates your faith! So do not let the desire to avoid the risk of failing become a barrier to discovering and developing the treasure inside of you! Doing so will only result in successfully becoming what you're trying to avoid the most – a true failure. Remember life isn't about playing it safe, but about not letting your faith fail! So go ahead and take the risk, live life on the edge and start to receive what only faith can reward.

## It's All Inside

*It's all inside!* Remember that jingle from the JC Penny commercial? Well, as it is true for JC Penny, it is true for you. It's All Inside!! Everything you need to manifest wealth is in you! You do not have to look on the outside because you are a co-creator with God! All you need to do to get what you desire is to look within and believe. You are your worth and are worth to be invested in!  Do not let anyone tell you different. Now it is up to you to decide to do all you can to discover, nurture and develop your gifts so that what's on the inside shows up on the outside! So do not wait another minute, go ahead and open up the treasure God has placed on the inside of you.

# Chapter 5

## Kingdom Key #3

# *There Is A Miracle In Your Mouth*

# Chapter 5

Kingdom Key #3

# *There Is A Miracle In Your Mouth*

*Death and life are in the power of the tongue: and those who love it will eat its fruit.*
—Proverbs 18:21

*Sticks and stones may break my bones, but words will never hurt me.* Remember saying this as a child during recess, at lunch, or maybe on the bus? Wherever it was, it was at a place where there was little adult supervision, and we as children had the opportunity to let loose. Ironically, even as children, we knew how false this statement was and the reason why we were saying it was because the words being said about us actually did hurt us, upset us, and caused us harm. As children we learned early that death and life are in the power of the tongue. With just a few words from our lips, we can build up people or tear them down. Inspire people to go for their dreams or convince them to give up. No matter how you use them, the fact is words are powerful and cannot be taken lightly.

Now, I am certain I am not revealing to you anything you have not already experienced either in your home, job, church, or school. In fact, I would wager most people know how bad it feels when they find out someone has talked about them in a negative manner. Amazingly enough however, there are a lot of people who are extremely oblivious to how much their own words affect them.

## Negative Words, Negative Reality

In the manifestation process, where thoughts turn into things, there is a stage when your feelings and thoughts are turned into speech, words, declarations, and announcements. Basically, whatever is on the inside of you is bound to show up on the outside. The Bible confirms this by saying, *"...out of the abundance of the heart the mouth speaketh"* (Matthew 12:34b). Consequently, what is said is a direct reflection of the thoughts and feelings of those speaking. Now these thoughts can be positive or negative. Whichever it is, I have learned once the words are spoken they affect more so the lives of those who spoke it, rather than the lives of whom it was spoken to or about.

What makes this a revelation is most people have the tendency to talk negatively about other people and themselves. I don't know why. It could be due to human nature, societal programming, their mental make up, or just a reaction to the pressures of life. The fact of the matter is most of us are in the habit of immediately focusing on their own and other's failures, faults and weaknesses before even considering their strengths, knowledge, and abilities. Because of this bad habit, many people live beneath their potential and never realize their dreams simply because of what they say. Why? Because negative thoughts lead to negative words and negative words lead to a negative reality.

## Cursing Yourself

*A man's belly shall be satisfied with the fruit of his mouth; and with the increase of his lips shall he be filled.* —Proverbs 18:20

Thoughts turn into things by what you say. You need to watch what you say about others. You cannot be certain how you affect people when you talk about someone negatively. However, you can be sure your words do affect you! Talking negatively about people is a no-win situation because words always come back to you. For example, most of us have experienced a constant complainer on one occasion or the other. If you are like me, you will try to avoid them whenever you see them because they can literally drain the life out of you with their negativity. They never feel good, they are never happy, they are always lonely, things never go their way, and they are always having trouble with their job, spouse, kids and/or money. The primary reason they are like this is because they are unaware they are simply reaping the fruit of their lips. Words always come back to you!!

You will never be able to improve yourself or your situation by thinking and talking negatively all the time. The same negativity you direct at someone else is the same negativity you use against yourself. For example, have you ever talked yourself out of a great idea or a wonderful opportunity? All you had to do was go for it, but then you found yourself saying:

*I can't afford it.*

*That's out of my league.*

*I'm not good enough.*

*I'm not worthy.*

*I'm not ready.*

*I can't do it.*

*I'm not smart enough.*

*I don't know where to start.*

Next thing you know you have talked yourself out of this great idea you were once excited about. You sabotaged your future and aborted your dreams simply because of your negativity. Once again your negative words led to a negative reality and now you must live with the unending pain of regret. Sound familiar?

In the rest of this chapter I want to reveal to you a better way. The fruit of your lips does not have to turn out rotten every time. You possess the ability to allow you and others to feast on good fruit from your lips!! Why, because there is a miracle in your mouth.

## Choose Life

*Death **and life** is in the power of the tongue...* —Proverbs 18:21a

Some of the readers of this book have forgotten they possess the power to decide on how their lives will turn out. Your future is not determined by random occurrences and coincidence. Instead, you determine your future! Like salvation, joy, peace, happiness, abundance and prosperity can all be yours by you simply choosing it to be. That's right! You can select how your time on this earth will be; either filled with death or with life.

*The power over the quality of your existence is available to you through your words.*

You may be thinking the previous is a very obvious statement. However, it appears to me many in society believe they do not have control over their lives. They demonstrate this by the way they live, act and especially, how they talk defeated. They walk defeated, live defeated, act defeated, and talk defeated. Defeated people living defeated lives expecting a defeated future. But it doesn't have to be this way.

The power over the quality of your existence is available to you through your words. Truly there is a miracle in your mouth, waiting to happen. Through a word, you can inspire yourself and others to do the impossible, see the invisible and touch the intangible. Consider, Dr. Martin Luther King Jr., who transformed the very fabric of America with the words, "I Have a Dream". Consider, the Apostle Paul, who evangelized entire countries from a jail cell through words written in letters to various churches in the cities of Corinth, Ephesus, Thessalonica, and Rome. Words are power and they are life. Words are potential miracles waiting to happen, and my word for you is to let it happen by choosing life.

Choose life because Jesus has chosen life for you and I. Did Jesus not say He came so we may have LIFE more abundantly (see John 10:10)? Did John not say the reason why God sacrificed His only begotten son is so no one would have to perish, but have eternal life (see John 3:16)? Are you starting to see a pattern developing here? God wants you to choose life, not death. So why aren't you doing this? Choose life!! I know it is easier said than done, so I am going to show you how you can do this immediately in your life.

## The Power of a Sound Mind

The decision to choose life over death requires you possess a sound mind. Words are birthed out of the soil of our minds. So it is highly important you be certain your mind is right so your words can be right.

> *For God hath not given us the spirit of fear; but of power, and of love, and of a* ***sound mind***. —2 Timothy 1: 7

What is a sound mind? The word *sound* in the Greek means *to be whole or healthy*. In this particular scripture it also takes on the additional meaning of having *self-control or self-discipline*. When you apply these meanings to the scripture God is stating He has given us power or *the ability* to love others and ourselves and the ability to have a whole, healthy and disciplined mind. In essence, God has given us the power to control our thoughts.

If we have the power to control our thoughts then we have the ability to identify and nullify any negative thoughts that enters into our minds. Just as we determine the health of our bodies by our diet and exercise. We also determine the health of our minds by what we meditate upon, believe, and say. This means the first step to possessing a sound mind is to clear out any negative thoughts we have about ourselves and start meditating upon what God says who we are.

What are we according to God? In the scriptures God calls us righteous, holy, wonderfully made, the head and not the tail, above and not beneath, rich, strong, blessed, highly favored, more than a conqueror.... I could go on and on, but I think you are starting to get the picture.

You and I are God's handiwork, fashioned in His image. Not only does God love us, but also He is *in love* with us, so much so He sent His only Son to die for us so that we may be able to live with Him. This is the truth of who we are, God's beloved, His sons and daughters, co-heirs to the Kingdom, and the righteousness of God.

For far too long we have allowed Satan to seduce us into thinking we are less than what God says we are. Thus allowing the feelings of guilt, fear and shame to mold our self-esteem and determine our self-worth. The Devil is a liar!! God has not given us the spirit of fear, but of power to overcome the wiles and tricks of the Devil. We are overcomers! We are winners! We are the called and God's chosen – no matter what!!

*You will never ever move from where you are by always refusing to face your weaknesses.*

This is what you need to start meditating on. The truth of what God says you are instead of the lies of people, society, governments, schools, politicians, and anybody who the evil wishes to use to deceive you. The Bible says, when we "*know the truth that the truth will make us free*" (John 8:32). Only once you accept God's truth about yourself as your own will you then have the freedom to have a whole and healthy mind and the liberty to live the life God intended for you.

**Stop Playing the Blame Game**

Another critical step in your decision to pursue life is choosing to stop playing the blame game. You know what the blame game is, don't you? People play it when they accuse someone or something else other than themselves for their failures. In essence, it's always somebody else's fault. It's always somebody else's fault for not being on time, not getting the promotion, not getting the raise, not getting hired, not being prepared, always being broke, always having a bad attitude, and so on and so on and so on. This occurs when people fail to take responsibility for their actions and refuse to admit it is "them" who need to change, instead of somebody else.

If this sounds like you in any way at all, stop the madness and start taking responsibility for yourself!! You will never ever move from where you are by always refusing to face your weaknesses. In fact, it takes facing your weaknesses and learning from them to get past them. Think about this. If you are saved, you would have never experienced the gift of salvation if you didn't admit to the fact you were a sinner. Once you admitted your faults and repented (turned away from them) then you were allowed to experience the joy of salvation. Well, the same principle occurs in the natural as it does in the supernatural. If you are to experience the better things of life, you must admit your faults and take action to improve on them or turn away from them all together.

When you do not do this you give away control over your life to someone else. You render yourself powerless in determining the outcome for yourself. You become a victim of people, society and circumstance; unable to make a difference in your own life. What type of life is this? Is it one you desire to live? If not, then stop playing the blame game and start taking responsibility for your actions. Once you do this you will discover miracles do not happen to people, but rather happen because of people.

## Changing Your Reality Is A Snap!!

After having read this you may be wondering how to start the process of gaining a sound mind and changing your reality to reflect what God says you can have. One simple little exercise to start you in this process is by wearing a rubber band on the wrist opposite of the one you wear your watch on. Then you snap the rubber band each time you discover you are speaking negative about you or someone else. That's right. Each time you find yourself talking about someone or yourself in a manner that is not uplifting, edifying or encouraging you simply snap that rubber band on your wrist. I bet you if you do this for thirty days, you will start changing the amount of negative speak because of the immediate pain associated with it.

I did this at my church. I literally passed out hundreds of rubber bands to the congregation and gave them the same instructions. Almost immediately I started to receive feedback. Many were astonished how negative they actually were. Some only lasted a week because they were suffering from so much wrist snapping. I cannot say that it worked for everyone, but it surely was an eye opener. I dare you to put this book down right now and find a rubber band. Don't worry, I will wait for you. I guarantee once you do this you will be totally amazed at how negative you can be and realize you need to start changing the way you speak.

There is a miracle in your mouth. It is now up to you to speak it, and then live it. I encourage you right now to start speaking life over your situation. No matter what it is, challenge yourself to see it as God sees it. See yourself as God sees you. We are wonderful in His sight. So go ahead and start speaking it and living it and watch how the miracles will just start to happen in your life.

Chapter 6

Kingdom Key #4

# *Ask and Receive Through Prayer Power*

# Chapter 6

Kingdom Key #4

# *Ask and Receive Through Prayer Power*

*Therefore I say to you, whatever things you ask when you pray, believe that you receive them, and you will have them.* —Matthew 21:22

The purpose of words is for communication, the exchange of ideas and information between individuals through speech or writing. As this exchange is performed a sense of mutual understanding is reached between those who are involved. When my wife and I communicate with each other, it is with the intention of coming together to make sure we both clearly understand each other's thoughts, ideas, desires, likes and dislikes. It is through this process we seek to strengthen our *connection* with each other.

Ultimately, communicating is about connecting. The purpose of connecting is to establish or maintain a link or bond to people at different levels. Right now I am communicating to you through the words contained in this book with the hope they will establish some sort of link between you and me. If I am successful in this, then both you and I are blessed because of the new found relationship made through this connection.

The strength of any relationship is based on the frequency of their communication. As I said before, most marriages fail due to the issue of money. Yet, they do not fail necessarily due to the amount of money they have, but because of their reluctance to simply *talk* about how they are going to manage, save, and spend their money. It is this lack of communication between a husband and wife on the issue of finance and others that ultimately leads to the deterioration of their relationship. You see, communication is key to the success of any relationship. No communication results in no connection. You've got to communicate in order to connect. Why I am running the risk of being redundant on this point? To point out the reason why many Christians do not realize the promises of God. *Their lack of communication to God through prayer.*

### The Purpose of Prayer

When is the last time you prayed? I'm not talking about the ritual prayers done when you eat or right before you go to bed *(even though many do not even do this)*. But I am referring to prayers that attract the ear of God because they are from your heart. You may not sound like Deacon Johnson during the devotional service or Sister Smith on the praise team. In fact, you may not even know what to say most of the time with your mouth. That's OK. The power of your prayer is not based on the eloquence of your speech or the length of your text. Instead it is fueled by what's on the inside of you!

Most people both in and outside of the church misunderstand what prayer really is. It is not is some sort of ritual reserved for certain times and certain people. God has given everyone the right to pray and the freedom to pray whenever and *however* they want. This freedom is because prayer is communication. It is our way of communicating with God and He with us. He desires that we pray so that a *connection* is made. God wants to link up with us. God wants this because once the connection is made; you will then start to realize God's foremost desire is to bless you. This desire is spelled out in scripture.

> *Beloved, I wish above all things that thou mayest prosper and be in health, even as thy soul prospereth.* —3 John 2

This desire of the Lord cannot be achieved without the connection prayer gives us to God. According to 3 John 2, we cannot expect to prosper in any other areas of our life until we prosper in our soul. Prayer prospers our souls because of the bond it establishes between God and man. The stronger the bond, the stronger the blessing. How can you expect to receive a blessing from someone without having a relationship with them? A relationship must exist on some level to experience any benefits from it.

Unfortunately, a lot of the relationships with God are one-sided. Think about it. You get up everyday with strength in your body. Live on the earth rent-free!! You have the activity of your limbs and are clothed in your right mind. Yet, you cannot take the time to say thank you. But you crave so much more from life and from God to the point of frustration.

Well, let me tell you how to end your frustration. All you have to do is to start praying!! The only cost to you is time. The old cliché is true. More prayer, more power!! So stop all of the excuses and start praying. Discovering the purpose of prayer is the first step of getting more out of your life. So kick up your prayer life! Pray when you get up in the morning. Pray when you take your shower. Pray on your way to work. Then you better make sure you pray when you are at work!! In essence just pray without ceasing and watch God move. I guarantee you will start to experience even greater levels of blessings because of the bond you establish with God through prayer.

## The Power of Asking

In the late nineties, there was a little book written by Bruce Wilkerson entitled, *The Prayer of Jabez.* As many of you know, it achieved tremendous success. It was number one on both the New York Times and USA Today Bestseller lists and over 9 million copies were sold throughout the world. In his book, Wilkerson pointed out how Jabez' simple prayer recorded in I Chronicles 4:10 was able to produce miracles in your life as it did for Jabez.

*And Jabez called on the God of Israel saying, "Oh, that You would bless me indeed, and enlarge my territory, that Your hand would be with me, and that You would keep*

*me from evil, that I may not cause pain!" So God granted him what he requested.*
—I Chronicles 4:10 (NKJV)

The key to the effectiveness of this prayer is not found necessarily in its words or its length. Instead, what makes Jabez's prayer so powerful is the suggestion that one could receive a BIG, HUGE blessing by simply asking for it.

Although finding great acceptance by most with his message, there were a few within the body of Christ, who were strongly opposed to what Wilkerson had written. They believed Wilkerson's message was too secular and materialistic. It didn't line up with their religious beliefs of what being "saved" is all about. Their opposition of receiving this message of asking and receiving revealed to me why so many Christians are missing out on the many blessings. They are afraid to ask for them!!

**Overcoming the Fear of Asking**

Most people have a fear of asking for things in general. This fear of asking is usually tied to how people were brought up, where it was considered rude or impolite to ask for what they wanted. In many cases one gets chided and embarrassed just for asking. As if they have offended someone with their request. Then there is the chance of being labeled greedy or ungrateful because of asking. As if you are not appreciative of what you already have and somehow wrong in your desire for more. Consequently, people generally accept whatever comes to them in order to avoid experiencing conflict that may result from their asking.

*We are led to think by asking God for more blessings implies we are not satisfied with the ones we already have.*

This worldly is also held in the church. Again, many believe it is rude or impolite to ask God to bless them. We are led to think by asking God for more blessings implies we are not satisfied with the ones we already have. We are shamed into a fear of asking God for our wants and desires; we believe we will somehow offend God with our ingratitude.

My question to you is do you believe God is so easily offended? I don't think so. In fact, I do not want to serve a God who gets so easily upset over my requests. Now, I am well aware there are a number of people who are a part of the body of Christ who lack the appreciation of what God has done for them. Somehow, they feel they *deserve* more for their membership. However, I do not believe God has a hard time distinguishing these people from those who are truly genuine with their requests.

Although it is correct and commendable to pray for others and their well being, we must finally realize the truth that there is nothing selfish in asking God to bless us. In fact, a major component of prayer is making our personal requests known unto God.

> *Be careful for nothing; but in everything by prayer and supplication with thanksgiving let your* ***requests*** *be made known unto* ***God****.* —Philippians 4:6

That's right. God desires to hear your requests. He wants to hear your hearts desires. Not for the sake of discovering what they are, for He knows our needs and desires before we even ask for them. But God wants to find out if *you* know that it is only He who can actually fulfill your request.

## Why Ask God

I really feel sorry for those persons who are stuck in the mindset that it is somehow improper to ask God to bless them. Especially, when the truth of the matter is there is no one else who is more qualified to do so. Who else knows us better than God, our Creator, our Sustainer, our Savior and Lord? There is no other person or thing in this world that we can look to completely satisfy our needs.

I'm sure you have discovered this to be true. How many times have you been disappointed by friends and even your own family members when you relied upon them to fulfill a need? How many times have you felt betrayed by people you expected to have your back and end up finding out they were the ones holding the knife? Then there is the job you knew would never lay you off because of how valuable you were to the business. But, then you get the age old cliché, "nothing personal, it's just business" as they hand you your pink slip and escort you out of the building due to the latest reorganization.

After experiencing disappointment after disappointment, looking towards other things and people to bless us, we often try to take matters in our own hands to bless ourselves. Yet, we are soon to discover this is a mistake as well. Simply because there is no way we can bless ourselves. No matter how much energy, time, and effort you extend to work things out for yourself, without God you will always fail.

*All throughout the Bible we find evidence of God having everything we need.*

The primary reason why it is impossible to bless ourselves is because of the universal principle; it always takes a greater entity to bless a lesser one. It cannot be the other way around. In order for someone to bless somebody else, somebody has to have in their possession what the other lacks in order to bless them. Just like you cannot expect a homeless person to provide you a home, you cannot expect yourself to provide something that you currently lack. When you try to bless yourself, by your own hand, you automatically set yourself up for great frustration and ultimate failure because you are going against this universal truth.

Have you not known somebody who is always busy working, scheming, and hustling for this and that, but never making any headway in their life? They are like a person on a treadmill, expanding a whole lot of energy, but going absolutely nowhere. The reason for this is because they haven't figured out they cannot give themselves what they do not have. They have to go to somebody who is greater than themselves who can provide for them what they need. Who else qualifies better in this than God?

All throughout the Bible we find evidence of God having everything we need. His resources and supply are limitless because everything on the earth, in the earth and above the earth is His (see Psalms 24:1). Why go to a limited source for your blessing when all you have to do is tap into the owner of all things for your blessing?

## You Are God's Property

One reason why many ignorantly choose to try to bless themselves is because they have either forgotten or are ignorant of who and whose they are. The Bible tells us we are not our own, but we have been bought with a price for the glory of God (see I Corinthians 6:19-20). The whole reason for Jesus' death, burial, and resurrection was to return us to our original state before the fall of man. This was done through an exchange. Christ's death in exchange for the souls of men. Once we receive this wonderful gift of salvation, we accept that we are not of this world, but a part of the God's Kingdom.

We are God's property. God is our Father and we are His children. Unlike many men in this present age who prefer to be merely sperm donors instead of caring fathers, God is not one of them. God is not an absentee father who runs away from His responsibility after spreading his seed. God's foremost desire is to take care of His children. In fact, He desires this so much that He doesn't want anybody else taking credit for blessing us. This is why He tells us He is a jealous God, wanting no other gods before Him. This includes: your family, your job, your friends, and your paycheck and yes, even *you*. Why go through the struggle and strain to bless yourself when you do not have to? Stop the madness. Let go and let God do what He wants and be blessed.

## You Have the Right To Ask

Now that you know God desires for you to make your requests known to Him, and He is the only one who is qualified to answer them, you can surmise, as His child, you have the right to ask. That's right. You and I have the entitlement, freedom and privilege to go to God with our heart's desires. As His children we have the right to ask for what we want. No one understands this better than my son, TJ. He believes that I, as his father, can provide him anything he thinks of. So anytime he thinks of something, he simply asks for it expecting he will receive it, no matter what. In fact, my son is literally dumbfounded when my wife and I tell him no. If you have children, you know what I mean.

Although my son will eventually come to understand my wife and I are limited resources, we who are children of the Most High must come to understand how God our Father is an unlimited resource. This is why God gives us the green light to ask, ask, and ask again. God will not get tired of our asking nor will He get irritated by it either. This is why we must accept our right to ask, but also learn how to ask BIG!!

**Ask BIG**

Most people suffer from a "just enough" mindset. If they could get just enough money, everything would be fine. If they could get just enough food, they would be satisfied. If they could get just enough love, then they would feel whole and valued. The problem with this mentality is just enough is always never enough.

So many people carry this mindset, because they have bought into the myth of "not enough" in the world. Not enough resources, oil, food, water, land and of course, money. With the help of the media who seem to propagate this myth at every turn, it is easy to see how we are convinced to believe there is simply not enough of what we all want in the world today. Consequently, this myth influences every aspect of our lives, including our prayers. Yet we need to be awakened to the truth of the whole matter; which is that we are connected to a God whose very nature is abundance.

As stated before, we serve a God who possesses no limits. Our God is almighty *El Shaddai,* meaning: He is a Big God who is capable of providing us with more than we could ask or think (see Ephesians 3:20). He can so easily promise this because in Him is infinite supply. There is simply nothing that our God can do or provide for us because there is nothing beyond the reach of our God.

What is also wonderful about our Lord is He is not a selfish God who seeks to hoard everything for Himself. He is not worried about suddenly running out of resources because He is the source. Therefore, our God is a sharing God and all throughout the Bible we see Him extending the invitation to partake in all He has. When God made Adam and Eve, He told them they have dominion over the earth and every living thing on it (see Genesis 1:26). In essence, God wanted to share with man so much so that He decided to give them a planet!! If this is not sharing in true form, then I do not know what is. What is even better than this is even after Adam and Eve sinned and cursed us all, God still desires for us to share in ruling all creation. This is why He sent Jesus to die and redeem us from our sins. So we could receive the original inheritance God intended. Didn't Jesus say He came to give us life and give it more abundantly? (see John 10:10) With this being true then, why are you only asking for small things when you serve such a great big and generous God?

When you pray, pray BIG by asking BIG. It is not like you are shocking God with your request because He already knows what you want before you ask it. I figure it takes the same amount of energy to ask for something BIG that it does to ask for something small. So why waste your time and God's time on the small things of life. Stop buying into the myth of not enough and tap into abundance of our God.

**How To Ask BIG**

Now before you go and ask God to win the lottery, or have a large, fat check suddenly appears in your mailbox, I want to explain to you on how you should ask BIG from the Lord. Most people have a difficult time with asking BIG from the Lord because they do not truly realize what asking BIG is all about. Asking BIG from God is not meant to suggest that you should use prayer to indulge your greed. One of the misnomers of the so-called *prosperity gospel* is the notion God wants to be our *super-butler.* In essence, if we pay him enough via tithes, offerings and sacrificial giving, then we can ask and expect from Him to fulfill our every whim and desire no matter how covetous it may be. Yet, this notion is far from the truth. Asking BIG from the Lord goes beyond seeking to satisfy any selfish materialistic desires. Rather, we should ask from the Lord the types of blessing that will enable us to establish long-lasting prosperity not only for our present, but also for our future.

Asking BIG requires thinking BIG. Thinking BIG is having the ability to think beyond your present circumstance and seeking systems and processes that enables you to generate wealth long-term. In short, it is *investment thinking.* Investment thinking leads to investment praying. So, instead of just praying for a job, you pray for a career. Instead of praying just for an apartment to rent, you pray to become a homeowner. Instead of praying for just healing, you pray for God to show you how to maintain health and prevent unnecessary illness.

*The hardest part about asking for something is waiting for it to come.*

You do not need the Lord to just bless you with something that will last only for the moment. Instead, you want God to bless you with knowledge, skills, and opportunities to allow you to manifest your hopes and dreams in and beyond your lifetime. So when you pray, ask BIG with the intent to receive a blessing that will not only satisfy your current conditions, but also enable you to leave a legacy that will impact the earth.

## God's Guarantee

Whenever my father-in-law, Deacon Lester McQuillon Sr., is asked if God truly answers prayer, his reply is, "God always answers prayer. Yet, it can be with a yes, no, or wait." The hardest part about asking for something is waiting for it to come. This compounded with the fact that God most popular answer is "wait" usually makes most of us doubt if God is even interested in answering our prayers. But, what I have learned through my relationship with God is that His "waits" are another way of saying "yes", but with time on it.

One of the biggest mistakes people make while waiting is giving up on the answers to what they're praying for too soon. This is because we as a whole lack the patience it takes to wait. We want everything to happen ASAP or *as soon as possible*!! We expect God to move on our time, and have the nerve to get an attitude when He doesn't. Again this leads to us questioning whether God will actually answer our prayers. The truth of the matter is we all could skip a lot of stress and potential sicknesses that result from it, if we would only realize and accept God's guarantee of an answer to each and every one of our requests.

> *Ask, and it will be given to you; seek, and you will find; knock, and it will be opened to you. For everyone who asks receives, and he who seeks finds, and to him who knocks it will be opened.* —Matthew 7:7-8 (NKJV)

As you can see, the scripture is emphatically clear in this matter. God guarantees to provide the answer once we decide to put forth the effort to ask. There are no ifs, mights, or maybes in the statement. Your answer is guaranteed! When you ask, seek, or knock, you WILL receive, find and have access to the open door!! Nowhere in the Bible does God compromise this Word. Even before the beginning of time, our eternal God resolved to always answer the requests of His people. This is why it is a *Kingdom Key*. It is a universal law based on God's truth that is principle in the Kingdom of God. Ask and you shall receive!!

## The Faith Factor

The reason God is so adamant about answering our prayers is because of the element of faith required in asking. Asking for your heart desires from the Lord takes faith. Believing God will supply whatsoever you are praying for. Hebrews 11:6 states, *"without faith, it is impossible to please God."* With this being true, we can conclude its converse is also true. In other words, *faith pleases God* and whenever God is pleased, He responds. God always responds to faith. This is what I define as the *faith factor!*

Whenever you want to get results from God, just display your faith by believing and acting on His Word. When you move by faith in any area of your life, God is completely and undeniably compelled to respond. He cannot help himself, because God is addicted to our faith. Your belief in Him gives Him what He desires and deserves the most: *Glory!*

Glory is the very nature of God. It is His essence. In Psalms 24, it declares that God is the "King of Glory". All creation instinctively declares His glory, except for man because of the freewill He gave to us. So when we, as freewill thinkers, decide to give God His due, He does what comes naturally to Him. He blesses us. It is this faith factor that obligates God to answer our prayers and allows us to have a level of expectation of receiving our answer.

### Set Your Expectation to Receive

*Therefore I say to you, whatever things you ask when you pray, believe that you receive them, and you will have them.* —Matthew 21:22 (NKJV)

Since we are guaranteed an answer to our prayers, our job is to have the faith to wait for it to come. The same faith it takes to ask is the same faith that gives us the right to have the expectation to receive. The key to ultimately receiving our answers from the Lord is believing the answer will surely come.

All throughout the Bible God promises "it" shall come to pass. Whatever your "it" is, you can bet the farm God's going to make your "it" happen. Delay does not mean denied. It just means become prepared. My brother, Ellington, always says it is our job to work while we wait. We work at becoming ready for what we're praying for. God's waits are only opportunities to prepare for the promise. Preparing and developing yourself is the way of keeping your expectation high during your waiting period so you are ready once the answer manifests. This is critical because only a person who maintains a high level of expectation will be able to see and receive the answer when it comes. On the other hand, an unprepared person with a low expectation will miss out entirely on God's final response. The worst thing that you can do as a believer is to miss out on the answer you've been waiting for so long because you did not take advantage your wait.

### The Secret To Accelerating Your Wait

Like I stated before, when God says, "Wait", He really means, "Yes, with time". The truth of the matter is God rarely says "No" to our requests.

Instead, He is merely saying to us "Not now" so we can develop and grow into the "Yes" He has for us. The reason why so many of the waits seem so long and the "yeses" seem slow to materialize is because we fail to recognize God's solution is usually right in front of our eyes.

Unfortunately, for many we were trained to always take our problems before the Lord. Now while this sounds good, it really caused us to detour from receiving our yes. We end up praying about the problem instead of the solution. By focusing on the problem in our prayers we magnified it. Whatever you magnify, will be magnified. In other words, you will never be able to receive what you chose not to see!! If you keep praying about the sickness, you will never see your healing. If you keep praying to God about how broke you are, you will never see your God given opportunities to become wealthy. All simply because whatever you magnify becomes magnified in your life. The problem becomes so large and intimidating in you until it literally blinds you to the solution that is most likely right in front of you.

> *...the secret to accelerating or even skipping your wait is to pray the solution, rather than your problem.*

So the secret to accelerating or even skipping your wait is to pray the solution, rather than your problem. Instead of praying the beginning, pray the ending!! Instead of telling God all about your trouble, start thanking Him for your solution! You need to learn to do exactly what Jesus did when he encountered the challenge to feed the five thousand with a boy's sack lunch of two fishes and five loaves of bread.

> *Then He commanded the multitudes to sit down on the grass. And He took the* ***five loaves*** *and the two fish, and looking up to heaven, He blessed and broke and gave the* ***loaves*** *to the disciples; and the disciples gave to the multitudes.* —Matthew 14:19

Jesus was able to resolve the conflict because he decided to focus on the solution rather than on the problem. Notice Jesus didn't tell God He didn't have enough food to feed the five thousand plus hungry people. Instead he simply blessed what He had and thanked Him for what He needed. By blessing the five loaves and the two fishes, Jesus showed us when we pray the solution God would not hesitate to provide it.

What end are you praying to God? The beginning, where you describe in detail your trouble? Or is it the ending, the solution, where you know God can and will provide if you would just ask for it? Stop being guilty for prolonging your wait and get to your yes quick, fast and in a hurry by praying your solution more than your problem. This is the secret of accelerating your wait.

## The Principal Thing

Once you start to apply this powerful key of asking and receiving in your prayer life, you will start to realize there is absolutely no blessing is beyond your reach. You will be able to put away all doubts and fears about God supplying your needs and many of your wants because of the absolute truth, God desires to grant your requests.

Of course the purpose of prayer is not solely to become wealthy for wealthy sake. Yet, if you embrace this principle you will begin to possess many things that you only once dreamed about. You shall become rich in all things! Therefore, my final recommendation on what to ask for in your prayers is wisdom, the principal thing.

In the Proverbs 4, Solomon advises us to seek after wisdom because once you get it you will also receive understanding. The reason why this is so important for you is because you must understand the purpose of your possessions. Also, you will need to learn how to best manage what you have. One of the worst fears rich people have is the fear of losing all they own. Yet, you do not have to live with this fear if you are continually seeking wisdom.

So when you pray, ask for wisdom. Seek her and then embrace her. For when you pray for wisdom, she will give you understanding and good judgment. Exalt her and she will promote you, honor you and protect you. When you walk, your steps will not be hindered. When you run, you shall not stumble (see Proverbs 4:5-13).

My prayer is for you to hold firm to the way of wisdom. For wisdom is the principal thing. For if you do, God will not only bless you, but also give you the ability to maximize the blessing. Amen.

# Chapter 7

## Kingdom Key #5

# *Fail to Plan, Plan to Fail*

## Chapter 7

### Kingdom Key #5

# *Fail to Plan, Plan to Fail*

*Write the vision and make it plain...* —Habakkuk 2:2

There are many who do not reach their Millionaire Mind potential because they lack a blueprint to guide them in the construction of their destinies. A map to help direct them from point A to point B. If you are to accomplish anything in your life, you are going to have to have to establish a strategy on how to reach your goals. In other words, you need a plan. I do not know who said the cliché, but it is so true that I consider it a *Kingdom Key* – when you *fail to plan, plan to fail.*

If you are anything like me, you have had some missed opportunities during the course of your life. You missed out on the chance to talk to someone. You missed out on the chance to invest in a great deal. You missed out on the opportunity to make a team, or to travel, or to get a promotion, or get your dream house. Some of you even missed out on dreams set right in front of you. You did not take advantage of the opportunity that presented itself because you found yourself without a plan.

Success or failure does not just happen. It is the result of either doing something or not. Missed opportunities are truly missed not when the opportunity presents itself, but it is missed in the moment when we decided not to prepare and develop what we need to take advantage of it. The surest way to failure is by not planning. In contrast, the surest way to success is by having and implementing a plan.

### The Value Of A Plan

Like the MasterCard commercial, one can put a price on possessing material things, however, the value of possessing a plan is *priceless.* The worth of a plan is such because anything is possible with a plan. I cannot tell you how many times I have received my heart's desires just because I put pen to paper and sketched out a process or method I thought would get me to my goal. I am a fan of planning because I know its value just cannot be matched. It is more valuable than money, food, clothes or shelter because you can get all of those things and whatever else you need with a plan. Every person of means will tell you the only way to receive and keep wealth are through a plan. It is the foundation of all success and the answer to any chaos that occurs in your life. The benefits of planning are so abundant and priceless that I suggest you stop praying for God to give you things and to start praying for God to give you a plan!!

Not only do I believe in the importance of planning, but God does too. All throughout the scripture we see God encouraging his people to develop a plan. In Habakkuk he tells his servant to, "Write the vision and make it plain…" In Proverbs, God tells us "where there is no vision (plan) the people perish." God not only advises us to plan, but He practices what He preaches by being a Master Planner. Just in the first few chapters of Genesis, we see God's master plan of redemption and salvation through the creation of all living things by His Words, "Let there be." Salvation is available to all because of the plan God started before time. Likewise, prosperity is available to everyone because of the plan God started before our birth.

> *For I know the* ***plans*** *I have for you," declares the LORD, "* ***plans*** *to prosper you and not to harm you,* ***plans*** *to give you hope and a future.* —Jeremiah 29:11 (NIV)

The whole Bible is our guide, our roadmap, and our plan to finding and fulfilling our purpose here on earth. God has placed so much value on planning; our response to God's plan should be to develop one of our own. A plan that coincides with His.

## Total Prosperity

In the opening chapters I talked about how God desires each of us experiences total prosperity in our lives as stated in 3 John 2.

*Beloved, I wish above all things that thou mayest prosper and be in health, even as thy soul prospereth.* —3 John 2

In this scripture we see how God desires for us to prosper in three major areas of our lives; our soul, our health and our wealth. Not until we are flourishing well in each area do we attain total prosperity in our lives. This lets us know prospering to God means more than just in our finances, or in our health. In fact, most persons are most likely experiencing success in one of these areas, but it is only in part. Having a lot of money in the bank is good, but doesn't bring much pleasure when you are too sick to enjoy it. Likewise for being healthy, but struggling financially. Yet, the most overlooked part of this trinity is the prosperity of our souls. How many people do you know who have money and their health, but are empty on the inside? Many attribute this to psychological issues; however, I believe it is do to the lack of development of their souls.

The primary message God wants us to glean from this scripture is the need to have balance in our lives. Balance between our soul, body and resources. However, if we are to achieve this balance we must then develop appropriate plans for each area. We need a soul plan, life plan and wealth plan.

## Soul Plan

As stated earlier the most overlooked and undervalued area of our lives are our souls. This is a major concern, because according to the scripture the level of our total prosperity is determined by the state of our souls. The scripture tells us everything else prospers *as our soul prospers.* This lets us know we cannot just leave our soul development to chance, but it is critical to create a Soul Plan that facilitates our spiritual growth.

*The scripture tells us everything else prospers* ***as our soul prospers.***

Christianity is more than a label, church membership, Bible study, or Sunday morning service. It is a journey of becoming. It is evolution in its purest form. Our goal is to evolve into what is already done in the spirit. When I am saved, I am automatically like Christ according to the spirit. However, it takes a lifetime of learning to be and act like Christ in my flesh. Consequently, I always find myself struggling with "flesh issues" that facilitates sin in my life.

The only way to confront these issues is by learning more about Christ daily and ultimately finding and fulfilling my purpose in Him. This means each and every person within the body of Christ must expect growth in their faith as time and seasons pass. Unfortunately, most in the church focus more on the sin than on the soul, which leads to a retardation instead of progression in their spiritual growth. This is why a person can be in "church" most of their lives, and yet still be ignorant about all the privileges they possess as an heir of God. They focus more on what they cannot do instead of learning about what all they can do through Christ. There is the saying, "whatever does not grow, dies." The church is in crisis because there are too many dead people filling the pews because they lack a Soul Plan to become spiritually mature.

### Steps to Spiritual Growth

I can hear you saying, "I don't want to be a spiritual retard. What are some steps I can start to implement in my Soul Plan?" I am glad you asked. The first step is:

*1. Assume The Responsibility*

Too many people in the church believe it is solely the pastor's job to ensure that you develop spiritually. This is one of the prevailing myths that plague the church as a whole and has neutralized our effectiveness on the world. The truth is *you* are responsible for your spiritual growth. This means you will have to go beyond attending Sunday morning service, an occasional Sunday school or Bible study. You have to step up to the plate and take charge of your spiritual growth.

The pastor and the church's leadership role is to help facilitate your growth like a coach does for an athletic team by making sure you have all the information needed to know how to play the game effectively. The problem in the church is too many people want the Pastor to be a player/coach with the intent of treating them like the superstar of the team. Then when the pastor/coach doesn't do what you want, they look to be traded to another team (church) or try to fire the coach (pastor) or go into early retirement.

I have seen too many people with major potential, waste it all because they decided to not be accountable for their soul's prosperity. Assume the responsibility to really become a disciple of God's Word. Attending an occasional church service or Bible study is not going to reveal the deeper purpose God has for your life. Stop putting undo pressure on your pastors to make you grow. Yes, we have a role to play, but all we can do is serve the food. You are the only one who can eat it.

*2. Focus On Relationship Instead Of Religion.*

One of the main reasons there is such a lack of interest in growing spiritually is because of *religion*. You know, the do's and the don'ts and the can and the cannots. I have found that because of this exaggeration on the rules and regulations of religious doctrines and denominations most people feel more imprisoned by God, than free. This is not to say understanding the particular doctrine of your denomination is not necessary for your growth in God. In fact, understanding Christian doctrine (resurrection, repentance, baptism, laying on of hands, tithing, etc) is essential for believers in order to create a foundation for their faith. However, you cannot stop there.

> *"therefore let us go on and get past the elementary stage in the teachings and doctrines of Christ and advance steadily toward the completeness and perfection that belong to spiritual maturity..."* —Hebrews 6:1a (AMP)

God wants us to move past the basics of Christianity and into a deeper understanding of Him. The only way to do this is by focusing on building up our relationship with God. The greatest gift God gave us was His son Jesus. Through Him, we are able to call God "abba father" which translates to Daddy. This implies that God wants more than your obedience, but your love. Loving someone is only shown through your relationship with them.

When you are in relationship with someone, your perspective changes from pleasing yourself to pleasing somebody else. If I am a good husband, I must learn what pleases my wife and then do it. It is the same with God. If He is truly your father, focus on learning about His likes and dislikes and what makes Him happy, then do it. Once you start doing this, you are no longer bound by the guilt of sin. You are free in your love. Not to say you will never struggle with sin. We are human and will miss the mark at times. Yet when you are in relationship with God, you will start to really understand God is not out to get you, but like a loving Father, He is there to love, support and forgive you when you fall.

The commandments of God are not there for the sake of giving you a guilt complex, but to show you how your life can be better than what it is right now if you follow His instructions. Yet, this revelation only comes with a personal relationship with Christ. Focus on your relationship with God instead of being religious. Once you do you will gain freedom to really live life to the fullest and receive all God has for you here on earth.

*3. Don't Settle For Average*

The last step I want to leave you with is *Don't Settle for Average.* Remember, if you want more, you must be more. You must be above the average Christian. You must make every effort to get involved. How? First, be more active and attentive in the services and Bible studies you attend. Approach them as a student approaches class. We encourage our members to bring notebooks and journals to each service to take notes from sermons and lessons taught.

Secondly, invest in the audio/video ministry by purchasing tapes, CDs and video of the sermons. I know your pastor may not be T.D. Jakes, Noel Jones or Juanita Bynum, but they definitely have something to say. It is a fact you will never receive all the information from the sermon at one sitting. Why not purchase the sermon so you can listen to it during the week and receive all you can from it. The more time you invest putting God's Word in you, will result in a greater appreciation for your Pastor and a deeper understanding of how God's Word impacts your life.

Thirdly, get involved in serving others. "Ministry" is defined as the act of serving. This lets us know that ministry is not just regulated to just preachers, deacons and leaders in the church. But we all were designed to be ministers in some form or fashion. Seek out ways of ministering through the ministries of your church. Believe me your help is needed and wanted. Ministering not only benefits those who receive it, but, even more so, those who give it. From doing it you will find out your gifts, increase you faith, and you will eventually be lead to your ultimate purpose.

These are just starter steps in developing your Soul Plan. Continue from here by adding to them. Track your improvement with a journal. Finally, stay committed to it. Transition does not come over night, but in time. So give it just that and before you know it you will be moving from faith to faith and from glory to glory.

## Life Plan

The second major area that is essential to develop a plan for is for your physical existence while here on the earth. In essence you need a life plan.

Our lives can be broken down in three overall components: physical (body), psychological (mind), and social (lifestyle). So it is essential to make sure each of these parts is addressed in your life plan. It is also necessary to understand that because they are so linked to one another, the decisions you make for one area will most likely affect the other. So your task is to develop an overall life plan that provides a common goal for these three areas of your life. The following are some general tips to assist you in doing this.

### *Mind*

This whole book is dedicated to positively affecting your mind. Hopefully, you have already been inspired by what you have read and are beginning to change your perspective on what is, indeed, possible for you. As you go through this process of reshaping your thoughts, you must be aware it will not happen without its challenges. There will be all kinds of circumstances and situations that life will bring to distract you from your goal. Knowing this, you must stay focused on your goal. Keep the main thing the main thing. Do not let the small stuff affect you and cause you to detour off your path.

I know this sounds elementary, however, you know how difficult it is to stay focused on your goals. Shortcuts and get rich quick schemes are never ending and will always present themselves as the solution to your present problem, but do not fall for it!! One rule I have learned to always abide by is *"if it sounds too good to be true, it is too good to be true!!"* True and lasting success only comes through hard work. There is no such thing as a short cut. If you are to reach the next level of personal growth and achievement, you will have to sacrifice some blood, sweat and tears to get there.

*Start now in separating yourself from any negative forces in your life.*

Another hard and fast rule I follow is *"if it doesn't add value, don't deal with it."* Since you are reading this book, I know that you have the goal of developing *your highest self.* You need to make the decision right now to avoid, ignore, disregard, and pay no attention to anything and anybody who do not share in the same goal as you do!! Why? Because you must guard your mind at all costs! What you are attempting is a difficult task. This is why so many people choose to settle where they are at and never strive to move forward. So you do not need another thing or person trying to create doubt in your mind about your goal. Start now in separating yourself from any negative forces in your life. Yes, it will be hard; however, it will be worth doing sooner than later. Another reason to keep your focus is because of your most precious commodity - *time.*

You must live your life with the understanding that you cannot afford to waste your time. The time you have is valuable because you only have so little of it. The Bible lets us know that man is only of a few days and they are full of trouble (see Job 14:1). Too many people waste their time by having a laissez-faire attitude. Not caring what happens, how it happens, or when things happen to them. They just go with the flow. But as a child of God pursuing your goals, you cannot afford to be this way. You have a job to do and a goal to achieve!

So stay focused by keeping your eye on the prize!! Do not worry if things are not happening the way that you planned. The purpose of your plan is so you can get back on track when things happen – and they will! All in all, I have found it all works out for your good in the end.

### *Body*

Nothing reveals more to you about the reality of time than your body. Even at a relatively young age, I am more aware that my body is not what it used to be twenty, ten, or even five years ago. I am now discovering aches and pains that I thought were regulated to the senior saints. My feet do not move so swiftly as they used to. Grey hair seems to invade every possible place on my body. My mid-section seems to expand just by looking at food. Plus, I must now be concerned with diseases that accompany aging and how to prevent them from happening.

I am sure I am not alone in this sad revelation of becoming more like Clark Kent and less like Superman. Reality is life can easily become our *kryptonite* if we do not pay attention to it. Knowing the effects of aging, we must strive to develop a plan that maintains the health of our bodies.

This is where common sense comes in to play. First of all get your health checked out. You cannot develop any type of plan without knowing what you're working with. When was the last time you went to the doctor's and got a full physical? If you are 35 or older you need to start being checked regularly for certain diseases. Find out your family's medical history, as you may need to start getting checked out at an earlier age. Just because you look good on the outside does not mean everything is fine on the inside.

Your ethnicity also plays a role in your health, particularly for minorities in America. African-Americans rank the highest in almost every illness listed including hypertension, heart disease, diabetes, cancer, and HIV/AIDS. Unfortunately, this is caused by certain customs, traditions and traits specific to our heritage, like our fondness for fried foods. Therefore, you may have to consider making major changes in your diet and lifestyle that goes against your heritage. Yet, it will be well worth it when your reward is better health.

Secondly, you must look at how active you are. America is known for being a nation full of obese people. Reasons for this include the vast availability of fast food, the large size of meal portions, and our increasingly inactive lifestyles. Consequently, many have suffered illnesses and even early deaths because of not addressing the issue of being overweight. This is not to suggest that in order for you to be successful in life you need to be a certain size. Nor am I suggesting that God demands for you to be slim and trim. However, you must realize the negative effects that stem from being obese. If this includes you, start dealing with it. It is a shame to reach a level of success and not be able to enjoy it because of your weight.

One thing I desire is to be able to live an active long life and enjoy it! The only way for me to do this is to deal with whatever challenges I have with my body now. So when I hurt, I get up and go to the doctor. I schedule regular physicals. I always push myself to be active. I try to exercise regularly and watch what goes in my mouth. This is not to say I am in perfect shape and I could just jump up and run a marathon. However, I can say I am healthy and without any serious issues because it is a priority in my life.

In summary, make becoming healthy a priority in your life plan. Do what you have to do to prevent, maintain and work on right now. There is no way you will be ever be able to fully enjoy all God has for you if you don't. So start working it out today!!

### *Lifestyle*

Nothing impacts your body and your mind more than how you decide to operate your life day to day. With every passing moment, what you expose your body to and put inside of you becomes more critical in determining the degree of health you experience.

We currently live in an age where the mantra is *"if it feels good, then do it!!"* This is added to the growing ideology that we all have the right to do whatever we want, live the way we want, and act the way we want especially if we aren't hurting anybody. Therefore, we have a lot of people who indulge in many questionable activities and lifestyles that places their lives at risk for the sake of temporary bliss.

One of the main reason people will risk it all just to feel good for a moment is because they have no long term plan for their lives. The best suggestion I can give to you in this area of planning is to use common sense. No matter your race, culture, political stance, personal claim to sexuality, atheist, Muslim, Jew or Christian, God gave us all the gift of common sense. So use it!

Consider your present lifestyle choices and ask yourself the question, "Does it makes sense?" Were you aware that human beings are the only species on earth who are willing to risk hurting themselves in order to feel good? Every other species on the planet does whatever it takes to avoid hurting themselves. Are your choices and actions causing you to treat yourself worse than a dog would treat themselves?

If you are engaged in an activity or relationship that is doing you any type of harm, *stop it now!!* Get up and get away! Once you get away from it, you will realize how stupid and harmful it is. God did not bring you into this world so that you would have to live this way, or deal with what you are dealing with. He is just not that type of God.

Remember every action has a consequence! Use common sense and protect what God has given you. Do not risk your life over a feeling. Too many people are making permanent decision based on temporary feelings and living the rest of their lives with a lifetime of consequences. Address this in your life plan. Believe me your life will thank you for it.

Chapter 8

# *Creating Your Wealth Plan*

## Chapter 8

# *Creating Your Wealth Plan*

The last area that is critical to have a plan for is your wealth. It is said the average person making a standard salary in America will have at least a million dollars flow through their hands during their lifetime. That's right. You will most likely experience handling a million dollars during the course of your life! Accepting this as true, one must consider money problems are not due to not making enough money, but are due to the poor management of the money we make. Again, the primary reasons for this sad truth is the lack of a plan for the management of our money and for creating wealth. If you do not have a plan to manage what you have now, how do you expect to manage the riches you're dreaming for later? Success comes to those who are prepared. So start preparing! There are four key steps that must be taken in order to implement a successful wealth plan. They are:

1. Manage Your Debt
2. Tame Your Spending
3. Establish A System of Savings
4. Make Giving Your First Priority.

### Manage Your Debt

I am not one who believes you should not have any debt at all or having debt is a sin. The reality is you are going to acquire debt in your lifetime and some of it could be used to provide you access to your dreams, goals and to achieve millionaire status. In fact debt, used wisely, could really bless the Kingdom of God in funding large projects that would immediately impact the community, city and country it serves.

Debt becomes harmful when people acquire it unwisely and then lose control of it. There are some people who borrow with the intention of not repaying. According to the Bible this is wickedness (see Psalms 37:21). Yet, most people are not wicked, but are ignorant of how to properly acquire and utilize debt. Because of this they fall behind in paying their bills and risk ruining their credit and even going into bankruptcy. Everyone, at some point, has lived this situation either personally or professionally. In fact, you may be facing this stark reality right now. If so, be not dismayed. There is a way to regaining control back over your debt and ultimately canceling it, if you are willing to master your debt.

## Tips On Mastering Your Debt

Because so many have trouble mastering their debt, there are scores and scores of methods and processes available to help you manage, reduce and ultimately eliminate your debt. Because these methods can get very technical and involved, I dare not try to explain them all because it would require a whole other book for it. What I have found to be true in my life is if you are really serious about mastering your debt, you must possess at least one critical trait: the willingness to do whatever it takes spiritually and naturally to Master Your Debt!! The following tips will help start you on your journey.

### *Tip 1: Find Out What Your Working With*

This is probably the hardest step and the most powerful one. It is the hardest because it is always a challenge to reveal an area of your life that exposes your faults, mistakes, weaknesses and ignorance. No one likes to admit to any one else or even to themselves their flaws. This is especially true when it comes to money. However, it is necessary to open up your checkbook ledger so you can find out what you are working with. Therein lies the power.

Write down every type of income you bring into your household per month. Frankly, this is the easy part because you most likely have up to only three streams of income. The more challenging part of this task is listing out each of your expenses or bills. Again you want to do this per month. List those that have the greatest priority first. Such as your tithes & offerings, your mortgage or rent, your car note, insurances, utilities and finally any credit cards you have balances on.

You want to do this on some type of spreadsheet program like excel so you can always update it whenever you need to. Once you've listed all of your income and your expenses, then you want to figure out the sum totals of each category. Then you want to subtract your total expenses from your total income. The outcome reveals to you how much money you have left over (if any) each month after you've paid your monthly expenses. What you will find from doing this is how your cash flows during each month. It will also reveal to you pretty quickly if you are living beyond your means. If your monthly expenses are more than your monthly income, you are in trouble and need to consider making some major changes.

Again, if you find that your financial state is upside down after this exercise, do not let it upset you. This is not the time to judge or criticize your past actions and bad decisions. Also, do not let anyone else judge you or lay some type of guilt trip on you about it if you decide to share this information. What this is about is finding out what you are working with. Now you are armed with this knowledge and ready to start tackling your problem.

### *Tip 2: Do the Research*

Once you find out your financial state, you can start researching the variety of options out there to help manage and ultimately cancel your debt. As I stated earlier, there are many strategies and methods you can employ to master your debt such as debt consolidation, refinancing, payment strategies, paying more than the minimum of credit cards, curbing your spending, etc. The great part about this is with so many options out there to choose from, you are bound to find one that is just right for you.

The easiest place to start your research is the Internet. Google "debt management" and see how many sites come up from around the globe. There are also tons of books available on building wealth and eliminating debt. Two authors that I suggest are, Suze Orman, *Young, Fabulous and Broke* and Robert Kiyosaki *Rich Dad, Poor Dad.*

Always remember, you are not alone in your situation. There are many who have experienced this struggle. So ask around. Ask your family and friends. Find out what has worked for others. Also, take advantage of any seminars or workshops that are offered in your community, work or church. This is not the time to be embarrassed. You are on a mission so get all the help you need. So do the research.

***Tip 3: Good Credit is Your Reward***

A crucial point you must realize while going through the process of managing and eliminating your debt is the reward associated with establishing good credit. I always tell my congregation good credit is better than money. Why? Because when you have good credit, you can always get the money.

Whether or not your credit is bad is determined by your credit score. Your credit score is a number based on the information in your credit file that shows how likely you are to pay a loan back on time. The higher your score, the less risk you represent. The method lenders use is called a FICO score. A FICO score is a credit score developed by Fair Isaac Corporation. Your FICO score helps a lender determine whether you qualify for a loan and what interest rate you will pay. It also helps determine the cost of your insurance premiums will be. FICO scores range from 300 to 850. A "good" score is 700 or above. Again the higher the score, the better off you will be.

As you can see, it is vital for you do everything possible to reach and maintain a good credit score. Establishing a debt management plan and taming your spending are some ways to improve and maintain your credit rating. You can also help your credit rating by paying your bills on time. Just paying your bills aren't enough. Lenders want to know you are good stewards over your money. One way lenders judge this is seeing if you pay your bills on time. It all goes back to what Jesus said in Matthew, "If you are faithful over a few things, I will make you a ruler over many things." (Mathew 25:21)

I don't know about you, but I want to become a ruler over many things! This is the reward that is waiting for you on the other side of managing your debt. Do your research to learn more about credit, how it works, and how to improve it. There is tons of information available that can help educate you on how to maximize your credit.

*Mastering your debt boils down to two things, cutting down your overall expenses and bringing in more income.*

### *Tip 4: Realize It Takes Time*

Mastering your debt boils down to two things, cutting down your overall expenses and bringing in more income. Experience shows most people are able to find a way to cut their expenses before they are able to create a means to increase their income. However, no matter how much you cut, you most likely won't be able to eliminate your debt immediately. Remember it took some time to get into your situation, so it is going to take some time to get out. Do not get discourage while you are going through the process. Remember the reward at the end. Put your debt management plan in to action and commit to it. Then watch how it all comes together over time.

## Tame Your Spending

The second step in your wealth plan is tame your spending. If you have gone through the exercise of finding out what you're working with in your finances, you have probably realized your spending is a little out of control. One rule I have about spending is to simply not spend more than I make.

Although not easy, it is valid. If your monthly expenses are more than your monthly income, you are in trouble and need to consider changing your spending habits.

I already have a sense what you are thinking. "Right, Tecoy, all I have to do is just change how I spend my money! Sure, no problem!" Please understand I do not suggest this lightly. I know changing your spending habits is no easy task. In fact, changing habits period requires great focus and effort, yet it is possible. Ever heard of the cliché, "the only way to eat an elephant is one bite at a time"? Well, the only way to tackle changing your spending habits is by going at it "one bite at time". Which translates into tackling this big challenge with small steps. When you place your focus on the steps you are less likely to be overwhelmed by the enormity of the challenge. With this perspective in mind I want to present to you a couple of small tips to help you modify your spending.

***Tip 1: Give Yourself An Allowance***

The first small step you can implement immediately to help curb your spending is to give yourself an allowance. Today's technology makes it easy to spend beyond your means because of its focus on convenience. If you do not have cash, that's OK, just go by the ATM. If there is not an ATM available, just use your check card. If your check card does not have enough funds to cover it, go ahead and use your credit card. If you do not have a credit card, you can apply for store credit. Also offering you a 10 percent discount on what you purchased if you do it today. Sounds familiar?

With all of this convenience you can easily spend away your paycheck before it ever hits your bank account! So how do you counteract this? By giving yourself an allowance from your paycheck. What is the allowance for? It is for all of your entertainment, discretionary shopping and eating out. Figure out what is a realistic amount for your allowance with the spreadsheet you just developed showing your cashflow. Whatever you do, discipline yourself to stay within the amount you've designated. If you do this, you will be able to automatically start to live within your means because once your allowance if done and away with, then you are done.

One way of implementing this plan is by opening another checking account designated just for this. These days your employer can even assist you by depositing funds directly into this designated account right when you get paid. Of course, nothing is fool proof. You will have to use discipline and restraint to not dip into your main account once funds in your play account starts to run low. Remember to commit to playing by the rules and watch how your spending will start to adjust automatically.

### *Tip 2: Tame That Shopping Demon*

Another small step you can do to help you is to tame the shopping demon. You know what I am talking about. The little demon we all wrestle with at some point in our lives that makes you buy silly stuff for no reason at all. The best way to tame this demon is by developing a shopping plan before you go shopping.

This goes for the big and small purchases. Create a shopping list so you can avoid purchasing needless things. One of the best tools to use prior to purchasing your big-ticket items or when you are shopping for the holiday season is the Internet. Most of the time you can find the best price and the best store to purchase what you are looking for. Sometimes you can even get a better deal purchasing directly from a retailer's website than going into the store itself. The only trade off is having to wait for it to come via the mail.

Another small step in taming your shopping demon is to never go shopping when you are hungry or emotional. Have you ever gone grocery shopping hungry? You will buy up the whole store because all you want to do is satisfy your hunger. The same goes for shopping when you are emotional. If you are mad, sad, or depressed, please do not go shopping!! Why? Because you will spend up everything trying to make yourself feel better or worse trying to get back at somebody who does not care. Believe me, shopping can become very expensive therapy if you let it. Most times you will be paying for the bill long after the problem that caused you to go shopping is resolved. This is the perfect example of trying to fix a temporary problem with a permanent solution.

*Tip 3: Don't Try To Keep Up With the Jones'*

America is driven by fads and trends. If you are the type of person who foolishly tries to keep up with the latest and greatest you are most likely living beyond your means. Too many people fall into this trap because peer pressure to keep up and fit in with friends, family, neighbors and especially people they do not like. Another reason why people are so tempted is because of our society's competitive nature. Many times people do not feel good about themselves until they prove they are "better off" than somebody else. But this is a losing proposition, because there is always somebody "better off" than you.

Another point you must consider when you are tempted to join this losing battle, is that you have no idea what it took for some to have what they have. Remember the commercial with the guy on the lawnmower is talking about how great his life was because he had the new house, the latest car, and was even a member of a country club? The punch line of the commercial was the man saying, "And I am in debt up to my eyeballs, somebody please help me." It is a waste of time being jealous or envious of somebody else's material blessings. You never know what they had to do in order to get it. So do not get sucked into trying to keep up. Like Paul, you must be content in whatever state that you find yourself in. (see Philippians 4:11)

One area I find people making this mistake the most is in their shopping for clothes. It is so easy to run up a bill trying to keep up with the latest fashion fads and trends. Yet when people try this they end up buying overpriced items made up of cheap materials. Instead of trying to keep up with the latest and greatest when you shop, focus on placing timeless fashions into your wardrobe. What I mean by timeless are clothes that do not go out of style no matter what is in fashion. Items like a dark suit, classic dress and a good pair of jeans will never go out of style. Also nothing beats a great pair of shoes. Your feet are one of the most important members of your body so you really want to take care of what you place on them. You want to focus on quality instead of quantity. This means you will need to spend some money for these items. However, what you will find out is how much it will be worth when you are able to wear them for years instead of weeks.

Of course you do want to somewhat keep up with the times. So apply the same rule. If you are going to follow the trends, at least buy something that will last. As much as I love shopping in the alleys and streets of Los Angeles' and New York's fashion districts, I know what I buy there potentially will not last long. When I look to really beef up my wardrobe, I just bite the bullet and hit some of the pricier areas of Los Angeles and Manhattan where I will most likely find something of better quality. This is not to say you cannot find any quality deals in those other places, however, sometimes its good to go somewhere you do not have to guess if it is cheap or not. There is nothing worse than having to immediately replace something you just bought because it was of poor quality. Replacing cheap clothes tends to become very expensive. Although there are many bargains out there always remember the old saying, "You get what you pay for."

## Establish A System of Savings

After you have committed to managing your debt and taming your spending, your next step in your wealth plan is to establish a system of savings. So many people put off savings because they believe they do not have enough money to do it. Nothing could be further from the truth. Do you know how much money you waste in a week, let alone a month? I venture to guess a couple of hundred dollars per month. All on discretionary items we could live without are:

1. ***Eating Out*** - With the advent of drive through, take-out, and curbside it is easier and easier to choose to eat out rather than go home and take the time to cook something. The cost adds up. Consider limiting your take-out and saving money for something substantial in your future.

2. ***Premium Cable or Satellite*** - I am a true cable or satellite convert. TIVO to me is near the advent of the second coming. Yet, I realize it is a luxury, instead of a need. If just thinking about canceling your cable subscription sends you into fits all by itself, you may want to consider at least downgrading from premium to basic. You will at lest save $25 a month, which could go towards your saving's funds. Ask yourself, if you really need the premium package? How many movies do you actually watch? The truth may be you can get by without all the bells and whistles after all.

3. ***Grooming*** - I believe in looking good, and being well groomed. Yet, you do not want to sacrifice essentials in order to do it. Go ahead and get the touch ups, but learn how to at least style you own hair until you can afford to go to the salon or barber every week.

4. ***Landscaping*** - I don't know about where you live, but in California landscaping is big business because many people do not do their own yard work, including me. However, if you are not there yet financially, do it yourself. In fact, any service you can do yourself is an area you should look at in your effort to cut expenses and save.

These are just a few areas you can cut in order to start saving for your future.

It always helps to have a goal to help motivate you to do what is necessary to save. For those of you who are still renting, you should save up for a down payment for a house. Nothing else accelerates you towards your goal of establishing wealth than owning a home. There are three reasons I want to share with you why home ownership should be your primary goal for your savings.

1. ***Owning a home automatically increases your savings.*** Mortgage payments help build your net worth. Unlike rent payments, a portion of the money you pay goes toward building equity, for example the difference between the market value of a house and the amount still owed on the mortgage. As you pay off the mortgage, you owe less on the home and "own" a larger share of

it. Another advantage is the equity you build over the years can help qualify you for other loans, such as college and car loans.

2. ***Mortgage interest payments are deductible.*** By owning a home, you can write off the interest on your mortgage on your tax return. In many cases, this will bring you above the minimum itemized deductible, allowing you to write off many other items.
3. ***Additional tax benefits.*** The tax code is generous to homeowners. Not only can you deduct the interest on your home mortgage, but you can avoid taxes on the profit from selling your home if you buy another home of equal or greater value within two years of the sale. Also, Internal Revenue Service rules allow you to avoid taxes on up to $250,000 (or $500,000 if you are married and filing jointly) of profit from the sale of your home.

These three reasons alone provide enough motivation to establish a savings for a down payment for a home. A second goal is to save once you are a homeowner is your retirement.

Eventually, you will come to a point in your life where you will want to be able to permanently leave your job and enjoy life at your leisure. The most common way of doing this is by saving up for your retirement. For most, the best way to start saving for your retirement is through your employer. Most employers offer retirement packages as your 401k, 403b or an IRA, which you can contribute to automatically from each paycheck. There are four major benefits from retirement programs such as these.

1. ***Compound Interest.*** Most retirement programs are interest-bearing accounts that utilize the principle of compound interest, which means your money earns interest on the interest that it accrues, as well as on the original principal amount. Interest may be compounded daily, monthly, twice a year, or annually depending on the financial institution. Over time this really adds up. Even small amounts of money can double and triple in value given a long enough time horizon.

The beauty of compounded interest is it does not require any additional work on your part after your initial deposit. You just sit back and watch your investment grow. The only thing compound interest requires is time. The more time you give it, the more it benefits you!

2. *Tax Benefits.* Investing money through your 401(k) plan gives you the benefit of tax-deferred saving. This lets you increase your take home pay and decrease your current taxable income. Remember though, your pre-tax contributions are not tax-free, they are tax-deferred, which means you do not pay income tax on this money until you withdraw it from the plan (which should be at retirement, when you may be in a lower tax bracket).

3. *Free Money.* Some companies offer a match as an incentive to join the company retirement plan. It means the company will contribute a certain amount to your account for every dollar you contribute, up to a certain limit. In essence you can get free money! To receive the matching contribution, the plan may require you work a specified number of years. It makes good sense to take advantage of a company match by setting aside the maximum amount required to qualify for a matching contribution. If your employer offers a matching contribution, your retirement savings have the potential to grow much faster.

4. *Access to Contributions.* The contributions you invest in your company's 401(k) plan are designed to help you when you need them most: at retirement. But for unexpected circumstances, many plans allow employees to dip into their account balances before retirement. Generally, there are two ways to do this:

   *Loans*: When you take a loan from your 401(k) account, you actually take money out of your account, with a promise to repay it. You pay your account back the balance you borrowed, plus interest (a fixed rate determined at the time of the loan), through after-tax payroll deduction. In addition, as long as you repay your loan on time, you won't be subject to withholding taxes or penalties, as you would if you withdrew from your account before retirement.

*Withdrawals*: Withdrawals are a different story. When you withdraw money from your 401(k) account, you cannot put it back. Different plans may allow you to take withdrawals for different reasons. The most common withdrawal type for active participants is the hardship withdrawal. According to IRS regulations, to qualify for this type of withdrawal, your hardship must represent an immediate and heavy financial need and there must not be any other resources reasonably available to you to handle that financial need. The IRS recognizes four reasons for a hardship:

1. ***Medical Expenses.*** Payment of certain unreimbursable medical expenses incurred by the participant, the participant's spouse, or any dependents
2. ***Purchase of Home.*** Cost relating directly to the purchase of a participant's primary residence (excluding mortgage payments)
3. ***Educational Expenses.*** Payments of tuition, related educational fees, and room and board expenses, for the next year of post-secondary education for a participant, the participants spouse, or any dependents
4. ***Prevention of Foreclosure.*** Payments necessary to prevent eviction or foreclosure on the mortgage of a participant's principal residence

It is vital you consult with your employer's human resource department to be fully advised about your company's guidelines for the plans they offer before taking out a loan or making a withdrawal. Also, be aware there may be additional risks such as penalty fees, and additional taxes. Always do the research. You can never be too informed about this crucial area of your life.

It is never too early to start saving up for your retirement. In fact, the earlier you start the better off you will be. Go to your human research department and find out all of what your company offers. Most are savvy enough to even help you put away funds for a savings account. Having funds pulled out of your paycheck automatically is probably the best system of savings I know of because it takes away the pressure of you handling your own money. My motto is you cannot spend what you do not see. After a while you also will not miss it either. You are more adaptable than you think? You just have to get over the initial fear of starting. A good goal to reach for in your savings (including retirement) is ten percent of you gross income. I figure if it works for God, it should work for you. So just go ahead and do it. You will be amazed at the opportunities available to you once you establish your system of savings.

### Make Giving Your First Priority

I am an avid reader of books on achievement, success, and wealth. Nothing intrigues me more than discovering the many ways people have found to gain financial independence in America and throughout the world. My library is full of them. Most are secular in nature, written by people who are not concerned about expressing their religious beliefs. Yet incredibly each one has emphatically emphasized how giving is a critical key to creating and sustaining wealth. In fact, further recommend tithing ten percent of their gross income. In essence, they advise those who are striving to release their inner treasure, must make giving their first priority.

*The decision to be a giver should be made first, if you are to achieve your goal of **releasing your inner treasure**.*

Although I mention this last in this chapter, this step really should be the first one. Before you find out what you're working with, and managing your debt, and taming your spending and yes, even establishing your system of savings. The decision to be a giver should be made first, if you are to achieve your goal of *releasing your inner treasure.*

The question that immediately pops up in your mind is probably, "Why should giving be made a priority in my life?" In order for me to answer this completely I will have to ask you to keep reading on to the chapters dedicated to giving and the principle of tithing. But in an effort to answer in short, consider the fact that those who are rich in the world tells us that giving and tithing is a critical key to their financial success. Why? Because givers always receive. It is the law of seedtime and harvest better known as sowing and reaping.

Why is it Oprah Winfrey, Bill Gates, sports superstars, long lasting celebrities, and successful Fortune 500 corporations known for their philanthropic efforts? Because they understand when you make giving a priority, you create capacity to receive. This is the very thing you want to do and be known for – your giving.

The way to start being a giver, is to start tithing to your local church. Yes, there are many charities out there that could use your donations, however, they may or may not add value to the Kingdom of God. So first start tithing to your church to help support its ministerial efforts. Believe me, once you do, you will start to experience a pattern of exchange you never thought possible. Truly men, will give unto your bosom as promised in Luke 6:38. You will experience blessings form unexpected resources you never though was possible!

In order to not go any deeper into this allow me to end with this point. You will never go broke by giving to God!! God simply won't allow it to happen! Please read and reread the chapters about sowing and reaping and the principle of tithing. You will be amazed at what a dime out of a dollar will do!

## Commit to the Plan

There you have it. An outline for developing your total prosperity plan. I encourage you to really study this chapter and put this information to good use by developing your own plan for your spirit, mind, body and money. Write it down and speak it, out loud. Then commit to do it no matter what! Please understand once you do this, you will automatically attract trouble because you have started to realize your true value. No matter what comes, stay committed to the plan.

You must also remember your plan will take time. Things may not come together as quickly as you would like them too. I have learned my schedule is rarely God's schedule. But the old saying is true, *"He may not come when you want Him, but He will always be there right on time."* The saying is true for your plan.

> *For the vision is yet for an appointed time; But at the end it will speak, and it will not lie. Though it tarries, wait for it; Because it will surely come, It will not tarry.*
> —Habakkuk 2:3 (NKJV)

I can tell you from experience your plan will be worth the wait! For years my wife and I wanted to build our dream home. God spoke to my spirit one day and told me that if I would build his house He would build our house. Our church was about to start a multimillion-dollar building project and the opportunity was right there for us to work our plan. So we sowed generously and worked diligently to help build God's house. We were so excited by God's Word that we shared it with our congregation and many of them took hold of it and even received it before us. In fact, years passed, and the building was built, and it seemed as if everybody else got blessed with our promise. People from our congregation were moving into dream homes and some who were generational renters became owners during our waiting time. But we did not give up or start to envy others. We knew if we just stay committed to the plan, God would do just what He promised.

In 2004, my mother, brother, and his wife stumbled upon a new development of million dollar homes. Upon walking in the largest model they had, they were so excited about what they saw, they decided to call me. My mother then proceeded to prophesy the house that they were in would be the type of house we would call our next home. My brother and his wife agreed upon the word.

Upon hearing this, my wife and I decided to go out and look at the house they were talking about and instantly fell in love with it; however, we knew at the time we could not afford it. But by faith, we decided to let them know of our interest and gave them our information for the future.

Almost a year passed my mother became very ill with her third episode of breast cancer. People in our congregations were still getting their new homes and we were growing out of ours, but still being committed. Right when we learned that my mother's cancer had metastasized to her liver and brain and her cancer diagnosed as terminal – we got the phone call from the builder of the million dollar homes. They told us they would like to build the very house my mother prophesied to us on two acres of land we were blessed to acquire from my loving in-laws earlier in the year.

I wish I could tell you that God healed my mother and she lived to see her prophesy come to fruition. Yet, the Lord wanted her more and she passed on to her heavenly home. Yet, she passed knowing that God came though on His promise! At the time of this writing, we are in the process of building our million-dollar dream home on a prime parcel in a burgeoning city. We are living witnesses of God's guarantee!

*Commit to the LORD whatever you do, and your plans will succeed.* —Proverbs 16:3 (NIV)

Yes, the plan may tarry. But always remember that God has an appointed time for your plan to manifest. Our appointed time came at one of the worst times of our life. But what God showed us was it is all about His time and not ours. God does not need permission to bless you, nor, does He have to wait for everything to be right in your life to fulfill His promise. God picks the seasons and the time to bless you and He will bless you *anytime* He wants!!

I encourage you to hold on to your dreams, your visions and to the plans that God has given and will give you. Stay committed to them no matter what and watch how God blesses you and makes your plans succeed. If you never fail to plan, you will never plan to fail! So keep on planning!

Chapter 9

Kingdom Key #6

# *The Power of Partnerships*

## Chapter 9

Kingdom Key #6

# The Power of Partnerships

*Two are better than one, because they have a good reward for their labor.*
—Ecclesiastes 4:9 (NKJV)

Most of the keys presented in this book focus on what you need to do, for yourself by yourself, to unlock the millionaire potential within you. Applying these principles in your life will lead you to achieving levels of wealth and success you may never have ever thought possible. However, you cannot allow yourself to become enamored with these achievements because they reflect only the tip of the iceberg of your potential.

One of the temptations of attaining a level of success alone is the temptation to believe you have everything it takes to fully realize your goals and dreams without any help at all. However, nothing can be further from the truth! No matter how talented, educated, and yes, even anointed, you are, you alone are not enough to manifest the greatness stored inside of you!

If it has not occurred already, there will come a time in your life when you will go as far as you can go, do as much as you can do, and achieve as much as you can achieve. When the time comes, you will need to find a way to overcome in order to realize your full potential. How do you do this?

With the support of people who are willing to work with you to make your dreams come true! In other words, the only way to realize your dreams is through the power of partnerships!

Success done solo is no comparison to the success done with others. Working in isolation only exposes your limitations! Yet through partnerships you can achieve unlimited success!

### The Myth of Solo Success

In *The 17 Indisputable Laws of Teamwork,* John Maxwell states, "One is too small a number to achieve greatness." [1] No other statement can be truer. The reason most people never realize their inner greatness is because they have fallen for the myth of solo success! Granted, if you are anything like me, ambitious, focused, driven, controlling, and have the tendency to believe that I am just a bit smarter than everybody else. Ok, I am very transparent here! Then you know how easy it is to fall for this illusion. Especially when you are young and are operating in the prime of your life and in the bliss of your ignorance. There is no greater *ego* booster than to believe you and you alone can achieve all of your goals and therefore receive all of the credit for it!

Society does not help us in this area either because of the way they celebrate this illusion of solo success. In most game shows, only one person wins the prize. In most award ceremonies only one person receives the Oscar, or Grammy, in their particular category. Even in amateur or professional team sports, there is always a focus on the individual who is considered the star, franchise or most valuable player. So it is easy to believe greatness and its rewards are reserved for those who appear to not need any help or support because they are simply the best at what they do. However, even the best can tell you this is not true.

Even though it is without question that Michael Jordan was, and in many circles still is, regarded as the best basketball player in the world. He didn't start winning his championships until Scotty Pippin and Phil Jackson showed up. To their dismay, Shaq and Kobe will always be linked because of how they won three back to back to back NBA Championships together. Even the richest man in the world, Bill Gates did not achieve all of his wealth and success without help from his childhood friend and Microsoft's co-founder Paul Allen. As you can see through these examples, even those who are considered the most athletic, talented or gifted still need help from others in order to achieve their dreams.

## Unlimited Potential In A Limited Vessel

Now I am sure for some, what is being presented may seem like double talk – especially after having read in Chapter 5 on "You Are Your Wealth." So please, allow me to clarify. This key does not negate how valuable you are and how everything you need to obtain wealth and success is found internally and not externally. What this principle does point out, however, is the obvious truth that although you and I are full of unlimited potential, ultimately we need help in bringing it out, developing it and multiplying it, because we are trapped in a limited vessel. One of the perfect examples of this is Jesus Christ!

The first thing Jesus did once he decided to start his ministry was to go on a recruiting spree. Jesus fully understood he was an unlimited God, but he was trapped in a limited body during his season on earth. As God, he has the ability to be everywhere at one time. But as a man, he could only be in one place at one time. He submitted himself to the limitations of the physical laws of this realm. So in order to maximize himself, he chose to seek out like-minded men and women to support his agenda and ultimately use them to impact this world like no one else has ever done. Like Christ, we also must come to this realization. We face limitations within our earthly bodies that prevent us from achieving our destiny alone. Therefore, it is up to us to seek out partnerships with like-minded people who are able and willing to assist us in our goals as we assist them in theirs.

The reason it is impossible to achieve your dreams alone is because we all possess natural limitations inherent within. These areas can be summed up as time, talents and treasure.

### *Time*

I am sure you have heard the saying, "time is valuable". The reason for this saying is because of the nature of time. Since time is chronological, this means it can be measured. Sixty seconds in a minute, sixty minutes in an hour, twenty-four hours in a day, seven days in a week, fifty-two weeks in a year, ten years in a decade, and ten decades in a century. This is critical to understand because whatever can be measured can be restricted. This is especially true for humans. We have been given a certain amount of time of about seventy to eighty years to live upon the earth (Psalms 90:10). Therefore, time is a natural restrictor for everyone, because we all operate within a realm controlled by time.

*Talents are the natural abilities and skills that give us the potential for unlimited wealth.*

Time is not only measured, but is also progressive. Which means for every second, minute, hour, day, month and year that passes is actually time forever lost and irreclaimable. So when you waste your time, you are actually wasting critical moments of a limited life span you will never see again. Unfortunately, it is not until we are well into or near the end of our life's time span that we realize how precious time is. This is why it is so important to learn the value of time and to seek ways of redeeming and maximizing it. We can avoid having to settle for second best because we did not have enough time to achieve God's best for our lives.

### *Talents*

Not only are we restricted by time, but also by our talents. Talents are the natural abilities and skills that give us the potential for unlimited wealth. We all possess certain talents or gifts, yet we all are not gifted in the same areas. So while one person may possess great creative abilities, they may be short on certain organizational skills and vice-versa. The way we are affected by the varying nature of our gifts and talents is commonly described as our strengths and weaknesses. Therefore, the person who is creatively inclined, but lacking in organizational skills, would be referred to as strong in one area, but weak in the other. This is to say we all possess varying strengths and weaknesses. In other words, nobody is good at everything. So it is our job to find a means that maximizes our strengths and minimizes our weaknesses. Because if we do not we run the risk of not being able to truly exploit our talents due to being preoccupied by the limitations our inherent in our weaknesses.

### *Treasure*

The word treasure is used to describe how each one of us is able to create treasure or wealth for our lives. We are able to do this through the various skills, talents and geniuses we possess as expressed above. Because of this we are our best personal resource. However, though we possess this awesome ability, rarely are we able to maximize it because of our singleness. In other words, our treasure is limited because we are individually limited. In addition, we face the challenge of how to finance our dreams, whether pursuing higher education, opening a business, traveling overseas, recording an album or writing a book. Therefore, we spend our lives addressing the question of how do we pay for our unlimited dream as a limited resource?

Since we know that we are born with these innate limitations, with others to follow shortly after, how then are we supposed to achieve our dreams and fulfill our God given purpose in life?

## The Power of Partnerships

The solution to overcoming all of our limitations is through the power of partnerships. Two, or more, people coming together committing to achieve a common goal. Partnerships are powerful! They are God's answer to achieving optimal productivity! We see proof of this in nature where nothing produces after its own kind until after they come together. This law is true for all of God's creation from plants, trees, animals and, of course, humanity.

Not only is it a law of nature, but also just plain common sense. Two are better than one, three are better than two, four are better than three and so on. A group or a team always outperforms one person because there is only so much you can do as an individual. Accepting you are a limited resource is a humbling act. However, it is a liberating one as well because of all of the benefits that come with partnerships. The following is a brief listing of such benefits from the perspective of teamwork.

## Benefits of Becoming a Team Player

### *Takes the Limits Off*

The first benefit of working with a team is it enables you to free yourself of the natural restrictions from just being human. It takes the limits off of your time, talents and treasure through the opportunity to share in other people's skills, knowledge, abilities and resources. In essence, you do not have to do it all by yourself. If you do not know something, you now have the chance to ask someone else who is more knowledgeable about that topic. If you do not have the resources, you now can tap into other people's time, talents, ideas and money so you are not running the risk of draining yourself out completely prior to the completion of your goal. Working in a team also allows you to maximize your strengths and minimize your weaknesses. You can now focus on the things that you do best and let others who are more capable handle the rest.

The difference between the results of an individual compared to the results of a team is huge. In fact, the Bible backs this up in scripture.

> *Two are better than one, because they have a good reward for their labor. For if they fall, one will lift up his companion. But woe to him who is alone when he falls, For he has no one to help him up.* —Ecclesiastes 4:9-10 (NKJV)

What this is saying is, when you come together with just one more like-minded person and agree to accomplish a goal, you are more certain to achieve it because you have backup. Knowing you have backup also helps relieves the pressure and stress that comes from attempting to do great things. This is critical to recognize because of the guarantee of opposition occurring whenever any one attempts to accomplish great things. So it is comforting to know you will not be alone when the enemy comes to block your progress. Also it is great to have others to celebrate with when you have overcome the opposition and reached your goal.

### *Acceleration and Accomplishment of A Greater Goal*

Another strong benefit of working with a team is the acceleration that occurs in the process. This leads to the accomplishment of a greater goal than originally planned. This is a benefit I have experienced first hand with me and my brother pastoring the same church. At the time of this writing, we have been working together, as a Pastoral team, for a little over seven years. During this time we have accomplished many goals we truthfully would not have been able to do under normal circumstances. We have doubled our membership, substantially increased our giving, and constructed a multi-million dollar multipurpose Family Life Center. What is the secret to our success? Well, first there is God. Then, realizing the benefits of choosing to Pastor as a team, rather than doing it separately. I have no doubt in my mind we both could have successfully pastor a church alone. However, I do doubt we would experience the same measure of success if we pastored separately.

Our decision to combine our individual gifts allowed us to swiftly move past our original goals, and ultimately accomplish much greater goals in a short amount of time. This result is not just limited to my experience, but will occur with any group of people, who decide to come together as a team to accomplish a certain goal. The reason such a result is practically guaranteed is because of the power of synergy.

## The Power of Synergy

In order to understand better the power of synergy, one needs to know exactly what it is. Synergy is defined as "the interaction or cooperation of two or more organizations, substances, or other agents to produce a combined effect greater than the sum of their separate effects." A powerful example of synergy is found in the world of chemistry in which the periodic table is used as its foundation.

The periodic table is made up of chemical elements based on the periodic law. Each chemical element represented, such as hydrogen (H) and oxygen (O), are whole unto themselves. They do not lack anything and are created to fulfill a certain individualistic purpose in the universe. Chemistry is the study of these elements and the phenomenon that occurs when these elements are combined. When such elements are united they produce a totally new, powerful and unique element. For example, when hydrogen and oxygen combine they create a totally unique element called $H_2O$, which is water. This is, in a nutshell, the perfect example of synergism, one combining with another, producing a greater one.

*You may be good alone, but you are awesome together.*

Like the chemical elements found in the periodic table, we also are able to fulfill greater goals in a short period of time when we decide to cooperate and work with each other rather than strive to accomplish something alone. This is why in the book of Deuteronomy, God tells us one can put to flight a thousand, but two can put to flight ten thousand. It is through the power of synergy we experience God-like results.

I can truly say my brother and I have experienced this from both working as a team and by recruiting other strong people with like passions, who have a heart for the ministry like us. It is because of this act we are now considering expanding to a second much larger location within the city to help accommodate the exponential growth of the church.

These are just two of the many benefits of choosing to become a team player. From just these examples you start to realize that we are not designed to work alone, but together. Again this is a critical lesson to grasp, because I can tell you from experience the old cliché is true, *"individuals play the game, but teams win the championships."* You may be good alone, but you are awesome together.

## Creating Effective Partnerships

Once you understand the need and the benefits of partnerships you are then ready to learn how to actually create them. The following are a few general rules you should follow in order to guarantee the success of your partnerships.

*1. Know Yourself*

The first and foremost requirement needed in this process is to be clear about your goals, vision and mission. This is important because you do not want to cause delays and detours by partnering with the wrong person. You also must be clear and honest about what your strengths and weaknesses are. Why? So you will not waste time partnering with people who are strong in the same areas you are. Your goal is to match your weaknesses with someone else's strengths so the partnerships can be as fruitful as they can be. As you can imagine, this step requires letting go of any false pride, so your ego will not get into the way of honestly assessing yourself.

*2. Seek Out Agreement*

Amos 3:3 asks the question, *"Can two walk together, unless they are agreed?"* Of course the answer is an emphatic NO! Therefore, it is necessary you seek out people for your team who are in agreement with your goals, vision and mission. They must share your aspirations and be willing to support you in achieving them even when it means temporarily placing their goals on hold. If not, there will always be a tug-of-war between their agenda and your dreams. I cannot overstate the importance of this step in creating effective partnerships. If this step is overlooked you will spend your time competing instead of completing.

*3. Match Partners with Purposes*

Initially you will want to partner with the people you normally hang out with because they are either your friends or family. However, this may not be the best choice for you. You must realize there are different partners for different purposes. For example, you may not want to partner with family for a business purpose. This is also true in reverse, where you should not expect business partners to necessarily become personal friends. Do not make the mistake of placing people in the wrong position for the wrong reasons. This will only cause undue stress and heartache. Make the hard decisions early in the process in choosing the right person for the job, so you won't face an even harder one later.

*4. Make it Win –Win!*

Understanding the people who are agreeing to partner with you are sacrificing something to do so should make you want to make sure that the arrangement is worth their while. In essence, you want to make sure the relationship is a win-win for all parties. This can happen in many ways, but I find that the best way of doing this is by being respectful to them and grateful for their support. I have noticed how those in leadership positions take the people who work for them for granted when in truth they are not under any real obligation of doing so at all. Everyone has a choice! Respect them by sharing the credit when you win and stepping up to take the blame when you lose. Believe me when you do this you will not have any more problems when you are in need of more partners to fulfill your goals.

*5. Partner for Your Future!*

Finally, let me encourage you to remember your future is always on the line! It is up to no one else but you, as to how it will turn out and who will be involved in it. This is why it is crucial for you to be particular with whom you chose to partner with. You see, the people around you are either increasing you or decreasing you. This means, you may have to take a close look at who is around you and what type of impact they are having on your life. Are they enriching you or are they sucking all of the life out of you?

The type of people you want to hook up with are those who be, do and have what you desire. In essence, partner for your future! This may mean you will need to reach beyond your current circle of friends to partner up with those you do not normally associate with. It will be worth it. Understand, God has people positioned to prosper you in your future. It is your job to go out and meet them.

As you can see, creating effective partnerships will take a lot of commitment, work and hard decisions on your part, but it will be worth it on your part. The benefits of creating an effective team around you are limitless. Working in isolation will only bring about an early destruction of your dreams. But teamwork makes the dream work! Go out there and get your dream team!

Chapter 10

# *Mentors—Your Blueprint To Success*

## Chapter 10

# *Mentors—Your Blueprint To Success*

*As iron sharpens iron, so one man sharpens another.* —Proverbs 27:17 (NIV)

Having a team to work your dream is a great benefit to have. However, it is only a part of your partnership potential. No matter how many people you are in partnership with, if everyone is at the same level of knowledge, skill, and experience, then your dream will still never be achieved. Your team will just fail faster and harder. So what is the answer to this dilemma? Partnering up with someone to sharpen you! A mentor!

### Your Shortcut to Success

There is much talk about going to the next level, the next plateau and even the next dimension. Nevertheless, many miss out on reaching these subsequent stages of success because they have become too self-reliant. They think they know it all, or are too afraid to admit they do not because of their position. They do not mind having a team of people working for them, because it actually seems like something is being done. However, they are going nowhere fast by making the mistake of allowing *the blind to lead the blind.*

Consequently, you have a lot of people wasting time being stuck at a low level, doing the same thing, over and over again. They are hoping to stumble upon the key that will eventually lead them to their promised land. Remember, Israel in the wilderness? Yeah, forty years does not sound attractive to me either.

There is a popular saying that goes, "There are no shortcuts to success." And although I believe this to be true, I have found out there is an exception to the rule. What is it?

## *MENTORS!*

That's right! Mentors are the closest things to a shortcut there is to attaining your dreams of success and happiness. Why? Because they have actually achieved them! They have been there, done that, and received the t-shirt! They've developed the businesses, traveled the world, set the records, and made their riches and figured out how to best keep them. Within their experiences are the blueprints for your success. Maybe you ought to read it again, because this is the key, *the shortcut!* The problem Israel had in the wilderness was they were too afraid, stubborn, and proud to believe their mentors, *God and Moses* to take the land of promise. Consequently, they ended up delaying, and for many, denying their success for forty years!

Can we agree that you do not have forty years to wait for your success? In fact, I do not want you to wait one minute longer than you need to reach your dream! So what do you do? Take the shortcut! Find a mentor and follow the blueprint!

### Qualities of a Mentor

There is an old saying that goes, *"When the student is ready, the teacher appears."* Although true in many ways, many miss out on mentorship opportunities because they simply fail to recognize the *teacher* when they appear. This occurs because most people do not have a list of qualities to look for in a potential mentor. So here are a few so you can immediately recognize them when they do appear.

### *Accomplished*

Although this sounds simplistic, surprisingly, there are many who are willing to follow people whose only proof of success are their pipe dreams. However, you cannot allow yourself to be fooled by people who are more talk than walk. You want to choose a person who has the expertise and experience required to guide you in the direction you wish to go. Therefore, make sure your potential mentor's success is not a secret. You want a mentor who is known for their accomplishments and is considered a star player in their field!! So in your search do not settle for less than the best!

*The goal of mentoring is to advance you from one level of development to another.*

### *Trustworthy*

The mentoring process is based on honesty and trust; therefore, it is crucial you look for these same qualities in a potential mentor. The way to do this is by getting to know as much about them as possible. What are their character traits? What do people say about them? What is their reputation? Remember most successful people have critics; therefore, you will need to rely upon your own wisdom to figure out what is truth. Determining a person's character is not quick or easy, but will be worth your time so you can have an effective mentoring relationship.

### *Challenging*

The goal of mentoring is to advance you from one level of development to another. The only way to do this is by exposing you to new experiences, people, methods and ideologies force you to think and operate outside of your comfort zone. For many, this can be very stressful, because it means doing things you do not necessarily understand or feel comfortable doing. But a good mentor will need to test and challenge your convictions to see how strong they are and to expose their weaknesses. The mentoring process is not for the faint of heart or mind. Everything you believe and have learned will be tested.

### *Patient and Encouraging*

Sooner or later you will make mistakes out of fear, ignorance, or doubt as you undergo the mentorship process. You will become discouraged as you realize how strenuous the process of your development is. So it is critical to have a mentor who is patient enough to tolerate your mistakes and wise enough to know your development will take time. Therefore, look for mature people who know how to celebrate when you win, but even more important, encourage you when you lose.

### *Accessible*

Ideally, you want a mentor who is both willing and able to set aside time specifically for the purpose of mentoring you one-on-one. You want total access to them so you can communicate with them regularly and have opportunity to "hang out" while they are doing what they are training you for. The advantage of having this type of access is the fact the best lessons learned are those that are caught through observations and experiences, rather than taught in a classroom or in an interview. Most of the time people get into a habit of doing a particular action that is significant to their success, which seems insignificant to them. Thus they will often times forget to verbalize it. Therefore, you want to take advantage of any and every opportunity to observe them in action so you can hear and see what was not said.

### *What about people who aren't accessible?*

There are times when you may not be able to get one-on-one time with the person you want to mentor you. In fact, you will find in many cases, you cannot just simply walk up to a person and convince them into being your mentor, especially if they are a celebrity or famous in their profession. Therefore, you will need to be open to the opportunities they offer to impart their wisdom to you. Purchase their books, tapes and CD's. Attend their seminars and workshops they present during the year. Be open to participating on a web conference or a teleconference they are conducting. Visit their booths at various conferences and expos in your area. You may even want to look at supporting them monetarily by become a partner with their business or ministry as a means of gaining a little more access to them. You never know.

To sum it up, just because you may not be able to meet with a person one-on-one, should not stop you from learning what you can from them. Never miss out on an opportunity to learn from successful people just because they are less accessible than others. Just because you may not know them or they know you, does not mean you cannot still benefit from their knowledge and have their wisdom impact you in a significant way.

## Criteria for Mentees

Just as there are certain qualities that make up a quality mentor, there are also certain attributes that are desirable for prospective mentees to ensure an effective and productive mentoring relationship. The following is a general listing of such qualities.

### *Humility*

Perhaps one of the most humbling acts a person can have is to admit they do not know something and/or certain things are outside their reach. This is especially so when the person has a measure of success and status. However, if you are to truly benefit from the mentoring process then you must become humble. This is not the time to prove how smart and accomplished you are. Remember you are the student! Your function in this relationship is to learn what you need to become more successful than what you are now. The only way to learn this is by admitting you truly do not know everything you need to meet your goals. No matter what you have accomplished in your life, you must realize there is always, always someone who knows more, done more, has more and is considered more than you. The Bible states, "God resists the proud and favors the humble." (James 4:6) I believe this is not only true for God, but also of people. So you must let go of your ego and suppress your pride if you truly desire to gain the favor of your mentors!

### *Teachable and flexible*

The job of a mentor is to expose you to new ideas, methods and people in order to get you closer to attaining your goals. More than likely, your traditions, customs and way of life will be challenged. What you thought was right may turn out to be wrong and vice-versa. Thus, you will need to be teachable and flexible in your role as pupil. Of course, this goes along with the need of being humble as stated above. This is not to say you should be willing to be taken advantage of or not keep your own ideology or identity. You must stay the great original you are! However, you do want to be open to new things, which is the very reason why you are in the relationship.

### *Loyalty*

The reason loyalty is so important for an effective relationship is because much of the lessons you are learning are caught instead of taught. Let me explain. When a person decides to mentor someone, they have decided to share aspects of their personal lives with them. They share their way of thinking, families, personal and business relationships, and how they go about making decisions. Their lives become so transparent to their protégés, they not only reveal their strengths, but their weaknesses as well. They take on this risk because there is no better lesson than the one that is experienced or observed. This is how one "catches" the lessons and thus really captures it and makes it their own.

There is no better example of this found than that of Elijah and Elisha in the Bible. Elijah was a major prophet in his day. In fact he was the Master Prophet of the School of Prophets. Yet, out of all of his students, there was only one, named Elisha, who would end up catching his mantle and ultimately succeed him in his role as Master Prophet. How did Elisha do this? Simply by being loyal to Elijah. Wherever Elijah went, Elisha followed, served and observed. In fact, those three actions provide a great description of what it means to be loyal to someone. One, who follows, serves and observes.

Loyalty is so important to an effective mentor relationship because it displays your worthiness of someone investing their time and wisdom into you.

Therefore, your loyalty should never be questioned. If you truly want to get the best from your mentor then it is up to you to remember how much you learn depends on how much you earn. So earn it by being loyal.

**Seasons**

One of the last things I must mention to you about the mentorship process is seasons. In the book of Ecclesiastes 3:1, Solomon teaches us that there is a season, time and a purpose for everything under heaven. One of the tough lessons to learn is this holds true for the mentors that come into your life as well. While some of your mentors will continue on for a lifetime, most will only last for the time it took to realize the goal. You cannot become depressed or disappointed with this because it is a part of the process. Many times you have to let go to move on. So what you do is thank God for the relationships He sent your way to move you along your journey and then look forward to who He has coming your way for your future!

As you can tell the mentoring process is not one to jump into lightly. In fact, if one does they will find out how sharp the iron of a mentor can be and most likely become hurt by it. Careful consideration must be taken by both parties to ensure they are ready to be committed to it. Of course there are some that will come naturally between parents and their children or a teacher and their pupil. However, you must realize you cannot settle to stop there because your dreams do not stop. In fact, the larger the dream the more help you will need. So, it is your duty to seek out these relationships until you reach your dream. Then you have the duty to be willing to be sought after to fill the role of mentor to those who were once like you. Once you do this, you then start acting in your divine self by creating a legacy!

# Chapter 11

Kingdom Key #7

## *You Reap What You Sow*

# Chapter 11

## Kingdom Key #7

# *You Reap What You Sow*

*Be not deceived; God is not mocked: for whatsoever a man sows, that will he also reap.* —Galatians 6:7

Is it not ironic that in every city, in every county, in every state across this nation there are neighborhoods literally filled with churches? I grew up referring to these religious passageways as "church rows". I am sure you are aware of a few in your city. The ironical aspect of this phenomenon is the high rate of crime and poverty is usually associated with these religious communities. All those churches - ranging from two to five on one block surrounded with gangs, poverty, liquor stores, prostitutes and drug dealers. Something is definitely wrong with this picture wouldn't you agree? One would figure with all of this church power in one area the community would eventually be influenced and start to change for the better.

Unfortunately, this is not the case for most of these communities. Instead of getting better, most stay the same or get worse. Now this is not to say the churches are solely responsible for the state their neighborhoods are in. In fact, the state of a community is a very complicated matter. So it takes many entities including churches, businesses, homeowners, entrepreneurs, district council leaders and more, dedicated to work together to improve the conditions for any community. Yet, the truth is most churches are not even invited to the table to discuss these issues partly due to the arrogance of the other organizations. Also because of their sad perception that churches are too heavenly focused to be any earthly good. How? By not having a strong enough economic foundation to support their spiritual agenda. In essence, churches lack influence because of their lack of affluence.

For me to continue with this premise, I must address the question, "Why are most churches poor?" The answer is simple. Most churches are poor because their people are poor. The reason why their people are poor is because their pastors refuse to simply talk about God's economic system of sowing and reaping.

### The Authority of God

*While the earth remaineth, **seedtime and harvest**, and cold and heat, and summer and winter, and day and night **shall not cease**.* —Genesis 8:22

In the eighth chapter of Genesis is the account where God speaks to Noah after the flood. In this conversation God makes four promises to Noah and his seed. God promises Noah as long as the earth remains there will be seedtime and harvest, cold and heat, summer and winter and day and night. As we know, from Genesis 1, things happen when God speaks. God's Word simply does not return void. In fact in Hebrews 11, the author confirms this in his exposition on faith in saying,

*"Through faith we understand that **the worlds were framed by the word of God**, so that things which are seen were not made of things which do appear."*
—Hebrews 11:3

This not only confirms the assumption of the creative power of God's Words, but also suggests the level of supremacy God's Words possess, which is absolute!! So when we look at what God tells Noah in Genesis 8, we must look at this as not only simple promises, but in fact as absolute truths established through the spoken words of the sovereign God.

An absolute truth is often referred to as a law. According to Webster's II New Riverside Dictionary, a law is *"a rule of action or conduct established by an authority, society or custom."* When something is referred to as a law, there is the expectation of the obligation of obedience on the part of all subject to the authority that created the laws. For example, everything and everyone on earth is subject to the physical law of gravity. It does not matter if you like or dislike gravity or even feel like obeying gravity or not, if you decide to not follow it you will suffer the consequences.

I discovered this, as a child, when I thought I could operate outside of the law of gravity and use the top of my grandmother's house as a spring-board so that I could obtain flight. As you can imagine, I soon realized, no matter how much I jumped off my grandmother's house hoping to soar through the sky, I always ended up with my rear on the ground. Why because of the law of gravity. It is absolute; definite, conclusive and unchangeable. What goes up must come down – *even if you believe you can fly.*

Just like gravity; day and night, cold and heat, and summer and winter are all laws established by God. How do I know they were established by God? Because David said in Psalms 24:1, *'The earth is the Lord's, and the fullness thereof; the world, and they that dwell therein."* This means that everything on the earth falls under the subjection of God.

Have you ever experienced a day without a night? How about cold without heat? I can personally say I have never experienced a summer without a winter. Why, because they are rules of conduct for the earth established by God. So if this holds true for those things, would not it also hold true for the very first thing God mentions to Moses - *seedtime and harvest*? I would think so.

## What is Seedtime and Harvest?

I am sure there are some of you who are reading this who wonders what exactly the law of seedtime and harvest is. Is it strictly a physical law of nature or is it a law that is applicable beyond the physical? First of all, I want to say once again, I am not a theologian. However, most theologians I have read believe the Bible was written to be taken both literally and figuratively.

This means we can take the Bible as an accurate account historically and also as a source of examples of life-lessons needed for success spiritually and naturally. If this is so, then we can presume when God promised there would always be seedtime and harvest for the earth's lifetime, He meant it as a law that is applicable on all levels.

In the Old Testament, this law is usually referred to in its physical version of seedtime and harvest because of the dominant agricultural culture of the time of when it was written. Yet, when you look at the New Testament, the term for seedtime and harvest is replaced with sowing and reaping. While this modified version still finds its roots in horticulture, the meaning of the term is broadened by its usage.

*There is a corresponding reason for every outcome that occurs naturally, physically, psychologically, and spiritually.*

Whether it is seedtime and harvest or sowing and reaping both are just different expressions of the fundamental law of cause and effect. This particular law states that for every effect there is a cause. One cannot happen without the other. There is a corresponding reason for every outcome that occurs naturally, physically, psychologically, and spiritually.

### Nothing Just Happens

*Do not be deceived, God is not mocked; for whatever a man sows, that he will also reap.* —Galatians 6:7 (NKJV)

The law of cause and effect implies there is no such thing as an accident or in other words, *nothing just happens.* One day, when I was driving my son TJ to school, he asked me, "How did Jesus make all these trees?" I thought about it for a minute and then answered saying, "He planted a whole lot of seeds." Guess what? Not only did this answer make sense to me, but it also made perfect sense to my then four-year-old son. If you want a whole lot of trees, then you need to plant a whole lot of seeds. You reap what you sow.

This is a truth is applicable to every aspect of our lives. If you desire to have a healthy body, then you need to exercise and eat properly. If you want to obtain a diploma, then you must take the time to enroll in a school, study and pass the tests to get it. No matter what it is you want to gain in your life, you must invest something in order to get it. Now if this is true for everything in our lives, then would not this same rule apply to receiving wealth? Of course it does. In fact Jesus makes this very clear in the gospel of Luke saying,

> *"Give, and it shall be given unto you; good measure, pressed down, and shaken together, and running over, shall men give into your bosom. For with the same measure that ye mete withal it shall be measured to you again."*—Luke 6:38

There it is, right in the Bible. Yet many Christians refuse to believe this and take advantage of the opportunities that this principle gives them. No wonder our churches are in such dire straights financially and spiritually. It is because most Christians are reaping the consequences of ignoring the reality of this law.

The reality of this law is it is always working. It cannot be turned off. For every seed is a harvest. Science describes this phenomenon like this, *"For every action is an equal or greater reaction."* This means there really are not any accidents because every action is automatically followed by a reaction. There is an *automatic harvest* for every action sowed. If your life is full of failure, then you must realize you are doing a particular action to cause failure to automatically appear in your life. Failure just does not happen. It is chosen.

All actions are choices. We either choose to do or to not do. Just like success is a choice, failure is a choice as well. The stark reality is too many Christians are ignorantly choosing failure than success for their lives: failure in their relationships, failure in their spiritual growth, failure in their careers, family, health and yes, money, all because they choose to do nothing.

## The Myth of Do Nothing

There is a prevailing misconception in American society that believes that there are no consequences to doing nothing. In fact, many believe there is a certain amount of safety and liberty of responsibility that comes from doing nothing. I call it the *myth of do nothing*. I am sure you have been tempted by it.

*Maybe it (he, she, they) will go away if I ignore it and do nothing.*

*I can't handle this so I'm just going to do nothing.*

*They don't need my help, so I'm just going to keep quiet and do nothing.*

*I'm too tired and stressed out so I'm just going to do nothing.*

*I'm going to do nothing and let the Lord handle it.*

Sounds familiar? It sure does to me and I would guess it does to you. Everybody has thought or said these very statements or something similar to it. Why, because everybody has experienced a particular problem, conflict or challenge that seemed too difficult to handle at some point in their lives. The notion to get up and run away is a common human reaction that everybody has. However, just because it is a common reaction does not mean it is the right reaction. There is a cliché that states, "Ignorance is bliss." However, we all find out, during the course of our lives, ignorance is rarely, if ever, bliss. In fact, in this age of information and knowledge, ignorance will not only threaten the success of your future, but could actually threaten your very existence. In most cases, there is nothing positive in deciding to do nothing because nothing begets nothing in return.

Jesus mentions several times the *poor shall be with us always.* The reason this is true is because just as much as Luke 6:38 holds true as is, its converse is just as true. *Simply put, if you do not give, then you will not receive.*

Paul warns us to not be deceived, God is not mocked or in other words, God's Word is absolute no matter what you believe. Do not fall for the myth of do nothing. Know there is a consequence to doing nothing. Why, because you absolutely reap what you sow. In fact, you are a product of what you sow. The question you need to ask yourself is what are you sowing?

### Designed for Your Benefit

Now I know you think that you have pretty much heard nearly everything on sowing and reaping. However, I want to let you know you have not heard it all. There are some new revelations about this ancient system that will bless you once you learn and apply them to your life!! But first you must completely understand and accept the system of sowing and reaping was designed exclusively for your benefit.

The whole principle of experiencing a harvest, greater than the seed sown, was made to bless you not hurt you. Some of you may wonder why I am including this somewhat obvious statement. Yet, I am aware there are some people who have been hurt by this teaching from abusive leaders in the pulpit. So I want to make it clear upfront to you, no matter what your experience was with this teaching, you must understand God designed it for your good!! That's right it is for your good and for your benefit. Yes, sowing of any kind can be challenging at times, but God promised us in His Word,

*"Those who sow in tears Shall reap in joy."*—Psalms 126:5 (NKJV)

God wants you to experience the enjoyment of your harvest of health, joy, peace, love and prosperity. And you know what? All of it is available to you through this system of sowing and reaping. Truly what you get is what you give.

Since God desperately wants you to experience a life full of prosperity and abundance, He makes sure you are supplied with everything you need to get your harvest.

## Seed, Power & Increase

The first revelation I must share with you is, God provides the seed, the power and the increase for you to get wealth!! Let me repeat this, God provides the seed, the power and the increase for you to get wealth!! The second revelation is if you handle the seed and power properly, God will guarantee you will have the increase you are looking for.

God has given you and me everything we need to be prosperous. The problem is we tend to ignore the tools our Father has provided us to attain financial stability and prosperity. Well, it is time for a turn around in your life. It is time you start using the tools God provided in this system of seedtime and harvest so you can finally walk in the prosperity God desires for you to have. But you must first understand the seed system in order to do this.

### The Seed System

*Now may He who supplies seed to the sower, and bread for food, supply and multiply the seed you have sown and increase the fruits of your righteousness, while you are enriched in everything for all liberality, which causes thanksgiving through us to God.* —2 Corinthians 9:10-11 (NKJV)

As stated before, God designed this process of seedtime and harvest for your benefit. God wants you to thrive in the system, not merely survive. In order to help guarantee your success God supplies you with the seed you need for you life. Now, there are a number of seeds God provides. There are faith seeds, words seeds, seeds of opportunity and there are also financial seeds. The financial seeds are any income earned, given or acquired in your life. A paycheck you get each pay period is a seed. A financial gift from family or friends is a seed. Any type of financial increase that comes into your life is a seed.

Now for you to fully grasp what this means in your life, you must realize who your source is. Allow me to clarify this by telling you who your source is not. Your job, is not your source. Your spouse is not your source. The government is not your source. Welfare is not your source. Your family is not your source. Your friends are not your source and you are not your source. If all of these aren't your source then who is? God is!! He is your source. I know this because God said it, in His Word!!

*But my God shall supply all your need according to his riches in glory by Christ Jesus.* —Philippians 4:19

Allow me to tell you, it took me a minute to figure this out, but I am so glad I did. It is so easy to become dependent upon these earthly things as our sole supplier for our needs. This is why jobs have so much power in our lives. In fact, it has been documented that many Americans spend more time at their jobs than with their families partly because of this belief. As a result, most people feel like they cannot say no to their jobs, for fear of losing their sole source of income. So what happens is our whole lives are dictated by our jobs. If we have a good day at work, then we have a good day at home and vice-versa. Unfortunately, we have more bad days than good days on the job which often translates into more bad days than good days in our homes.

Once I found how much my job was conflicting with my calling, I decided to follow the Lord's leading for my life to Pastor full time. Now I am not saying everyone should leave their jobs if they do not like them. However, life is too short to be dictated by a job. God never intended for your life to be controlled by your job, but by Him.

*Your job is a tool used by God to provide you seed.*

Then what is your job? Your job is a tool used by God to provide you seed. That's right it is a seed provider. One of the main reasons why you are at your job is to receive seed. The other is so you can be a witness for God. God chose your job, your occupation, your employer to bless you so you can become a blessing to others. You cannot be a blessing if you are always working or being stressed out about losing your job. You must remember your ultimate employer is God. In fact, you were born with a job, which is to glorify the Father in all you do. This is why you get up in the morning, to glorify God, not your job!

## Power to Get Wealth

God is not only the source of our seed, but he is also the source of our power to produce and increase our seed.

> *"And you shall remember the LORD your God, for it is He who gives you power to get wealth, that He may establish His covenant which He swore to your fathers, as it is this day."*—Deuteronomy 8:18 (NKJV)

Deuteronomy 8:18 shows us it is God who gives us the *power* to produce wealth in our lives. According to Vine's Expository Dictionary of Old and New Testament Words the word power means *might, strength, force, ability and capability*. When you take all of this into account, we can surmise that God has given us everything we need in order to produce wealth. There is no reason for us to be jealous of anybody else's talents or gifts, God has given each of us a unique mixture of abilities to achieve our dreams and reach our goals.

One of the Greek definitions that really excite me is the term *capability*. This tells me the resources needed to improve my life are already within me. We just do not have the possibility to become rich, but we are truly *capable* to achieve millionaire status. We all have a fighting chance!! No matter who you are, Black, White, Latino, Asian, male or female, we all have a fighting chance!! All we need to do is stir up those gifts, which are in us, and apply them properly to the established framework of God, then watch Him work.

Another way of explaining this concept is by substituting the word *power* with the word *potential* to make Deuteronomy 8:18 read like this:

> *"And you shall remember the LORD your God, for it is He who gives you* ***potential*** *to get wealth. . . ."*

The reason you need to look at this scripture this way is so you understand God is not going to just give you wealth for nothing. Remember nothing from nothing leaves nothing. You must actually get up and do something in order to get wealth. Yes, the power is in you, but it will lay dormant with you until you activate it!!

You cannot just sit around and expect God to drop money on you. He does not work that way. Instead, God wants you to work out your faith by putting it into action. I think James 2:17 says it best stating, *"faith without works is dead."* So do not just sit there on your faith, but take the initiative to act on it. This is the only way for you to realize your God given potential to create wealth. Knowing we have this God given opportunity to produce wealth, the next step is to identify how to maximize it.

### Developing a Giving Lifestyle

The primary way to maximize your power to get wealth is by developing a giving lifestyle!! Let me explain. Most Christians will never realize their wealth potential because of their reluctance to give!! If you have ever attended a Sunday morning church service, you know what I am talking about. That's right tithes and offering time!!

For most American churches, the tithes and offering period is the most dreaded time of the worship service. In fact, it is not even considered by many a part of the service, but instead an interruption in the service's flow. Consequently, most offerings processionals resemble more like funeral processionals accompanied with a whole lot of anxiety, sadness, fear and grief instead of with the joy that should be associated it. This attitude towards this time of worship is prevalent in our churches because people's natural negative feelings towards giving are rarely challenged with the truth of gaining wealth. Unfortunately, people either do not recognize or comprehend this time of giving is not just a necessary evil that should be grudgingly tolerated, but a tremendous opportunity to participate in God's seed system through their giving.

You can never go wrong giving, especially to a church where it is evident the Lord dwells in it. Yet, it is proven on every Sunday morning most people have a hard time doing so. Have you ever wondered why it is so hard to give to God? Why you seem to have an internal civil war occur when you are challenged to give beyond your comfort zone in worship? I have and have discovered why? The reason why is simply because it is God's will for us to develop a giving lifestyle.

Developing a giving lifestyle is essential in tapping into your treasure and ultimately fulfilling God's purpose for your life. In the Gospel of Luke Jesus puts it this way:

> *"Give, and it will be given to you: good measure, pressed down, shaken together, and running over will be put into your bosom. For with the same measure that you use, it will be measured back to you."*—Luke 6:38 (NKJV)

If you have ever attended a Sunday morning service, you have most likely heard this scripture being used at tithes and offering time. However, what is lost upon many is the much broader scope this scripture holds beyond the practice of giving tithes and offerings. Look at this same scripture in the Message translation.

> *Give away your life; you'll find life given back, but not merely given back—given back with bonus and blessing. Giving, not getting, is the way. Generosity begets generosity."*
> —Luke 6:38 (MSG)

Do you see the broader scope of the scripture now? Basically it is *givers get.* That's right givers get!! Now this notion seems pretty ludicrous to those who are poverty conscious. Those with this mindset believe there is a limited amount of resources in the world. Giving anything away whether it is time, money, or friendship is a wasted effort because they believe they will never get it back.

*...people who practice generosity often experience the more they give the more they received.*

However, for those who are abundance conscious understand there is no such thing as a limited amount of anything because God controls it all and will give you what you need and desire, if you believe. Thus, giving for them is a method of adding and multiplying their resources rather than subtracting from them. In fact people who practice generosity often experience the more they give the more they received. This is the bonus and the blessing the above scripture refers to.

I can readily testify to the bonus and blessings that giving benefits the giver. My wife and I have always been strong givers in the church and community. We tithe regularly and donate our time, and talents to the Lord freely. God has always blessed us through our ups and downs. However, we never experienced the blessings that we have until we started to give generously.

One thing I have noticed is, when God wants to bless you He will create a need for seed. That is an opportunity for you to sow. The reason for this is because of this key principle of sowing and reaping. The need God created was the mandate for our church to construct a multimillion-dollar family life center in honor of my father, Dr. Robert Porter, the founder of our church. So we launched into a capital campaign to raise funds for the new Dr. Robert Porter Center. I can tell you now, it wasn't an easy road, but God did it. In

October of 2003, we walked into our new center equipped with a full court gymnasium, administrative wing, educational wing, and state of the art stage, sound and lighting. To God Be the Glory!!

But in order for us to accomplish this tremendous work for the Lord, the church family was challenged to give above and beyond our normal tithes and offerings. As one of the Pastors of our church, we certainly had to do it to set the example. So we did. My wife and I gave thousands upon thousands of dollars to the project, but we never experienced any loss at all. In fact, all we have experienced is abundance and increase. God just seemed to multiply our money, and substantially decrease our debt. Truly the scripture proved right in my experience – *generosity begets generosity.*

### Barrier to Generosity

If the principle of sowing and reaping is true, then there is the question of, "Why aren't more people, especially Christians, doing it? Unfortunately, the answer is simple; it is because of their love of money.

> *For the love of money is the root of all evil: which while some coveted after, they have erred from the faith, and pierced themselves through with many sorrows.* —I Timothy 6:10

It is hard to not be in love with money, especially in America whose whole system is built on consumerism. Every where you look, whether it be on the television, radio, or billboards somebody somewhere is trying to sell you the next big thing, or the latest fad or trend with claims, you cannot live without. Of course, you cannot buy any of these things without money. So without even being aware of it, we slip into a covetous mindset and start to devote all of our efforts to making enough money so that we can pursue the acquisition of these things. In other words, we dive into the world of materialism. We become totally devoted to attaining material worth. So we work forty to sixty hours a week just so that we can buy stuff we do not need and really cannot afford. Why, because we are led to believe that this "stuff" defines who and what we are. Plus it just down right makes us feel good about ourselves.

Think about it. How many times have you based your self-worth upon the balance in your bank account, the car you drive, the neighborhood in which you live, or the clothes that you wear? Worst yet, how many times have you judged a person and their self-worth based upon these same things? I know I am guilty and probably most of you who are reading my confession, are guilty of this too. Why? Because we have been taught to place a greater value on material wealth and possessions at the expense of anything else – *even our commitment to God.* Knowing this, there is no wonder why many hold such a strong disdain to those who ask for us to "give" away our money each Sunday morning.

**There's Always a Cost**

There is no question people love money and what it can get for them. Yet, what is equally true is the terrible price many people pay for this love. Paul tells us, for those who choose to chase after it have *"erred from the faith, and pierced themselves through with many sorrows".* (I Timothy 6:10) Many of you know no other words ring any truer. This love hurts!! It is painful because there is always a cost that comes with it that eventually causes sorrow. Bankruptcies, divorces, bad credit, poverty, and depression are just a few of the many sorrows the *"love of money"* brings. Not to mention the unfortunate results of drug use, abuse and suicide that usually follows depression.

Paul tells us, the reason for these sorrows is due to the misplacing of our faith. Instead of placing our faith in God, we place it in money or the things it buys us. This is an error; we try to make these things that are dead and temporary, fill a deep seated-need that is alive and spiritual. It is like trying to put a square peg into a round hole. It just won't fit right, even if you force it. Consequently, there is pain and sorrow.

Many have fallen for the trap of loving money because of the common belief that money equals success. Unfortunately, this belief proves to be more false than true. This is not to say that money is not essential to achieving success in this world. One needs affluence to have influence. Yet, it is not the sole measurement of success.

> *For what shall it profit a man, if he shall gain the whole world, and lose his own soul?* —Mark 8:36

The above scripture warns us against the dangerous pursuit of having the perspective of gaining success though wealth. Mark tells us there is no profit in this definition of success due to the possibility of becoming a slave to the very thing we are trying to master. This especially holds true for those who are already "wealthy" because of their already strong ties to having money. If you need proof just look at the politicians involved in the savings and loan scandal, or the number of corporate executives recently charged of committing stock fraud. These rich and powerful people risked everything they have by committing illegal acts because of their greed!!

***The condition of your soul directly effects the decisions you make during your life.***

Consider the once famous, now infamous Martha Stewart, who was convicted on charges of insider trading. A self-made millionaire risking her multi-million dollar empire just for a tip that would only save her thousands. I don't know about you, but I would not risk millions just to save a few thousand. I guess King Solomon, the richest monarch in ancient Israel was right when he said,

> *"Whoever loves money never has enough; whoever loves wealth is never satisfied with his income"*—Ecclesiastes 5:10 (NIV)

St. Mark also lets us know you can gain the world—for a price. Unfortunately, the price is a costly one for it is your soul. Your soul is the essence of who you are. It is the very core of your being. The condition of your soul directly effects the decisions you make during your life. If your soul is sold out to the world and its possessions, then you are constantly positioning yourself to experience disappointments after disappointments in your life. Just ask the rich young ruler. According to the story, the young man knew he was missing something in his life although he was rich, successful and powerful. So, he goes seeking after Jesus asking for what he is missing. Jesus replies stating that the young ruler should give away all he has and to follow Him.

*But when the young man heard that saying, he went away sorrowful: for he had great possessions.* —Matthew 19:22

The young man was tied to his possessions so much so he could not see the greater blessing that was right in front of him. Being with Christ. Many of us may frown upon the young ruler for his response to Jesus, but how many times have we responded in the same way because of what we possess? Just like the rich young ruler, we have sealed the fate of our destiny with sorrow because of the state of our souls.

Realizing the sorrows of loving money, it would seem it is safer for us to never become wealthy. But I believe this is an unhealthy perspective to have as a Christian for how are we to accomplish God's will on earth as it is in heaven if we are broke? Success is not just about having money, but about having the type of character that releases God to entrust you with money to do His Will.

### A Matter of the Heart

Developing a giving lifestyle is not a matter of money, but a matter of the heart. It is the condition of your heart that determines your success with attaining and maintaining wealth. Matthew gives us more insight about this truth when he said,

*"For where your treasure is, there will your heart be also."* —Matthew 6:21

Many people have a problem with giving because their money is where their heart is. They simply love it more than God. I know this to be true, because I am usually the one appointed to the task of asking people to give. There is no other subject that causes such conflict, angst and anxiety than the subject of giving money to God. Sunday after Sunday people make the same choice the rich, young ruler made and walks away from their greatness in sorrow because they treasure money more than they treasure God.

Ironically, God does not need our money. God is not broke, busted or disgusted. He does not need a loan from us of any kind. He simply owns it all. One may wonder since this is true, then why does he put us through such turmoil by asking us to give away what He already has so much of? The answer is simple.

*God wants your heart.*

God wants you to treasure Him as much as He treasures us. Just think about how much God loves us. Now think about how much God loves you!!

*Yes, you!*

*The real you!*

*The sacred you!*

*The vulnerable you!*

The "you" you are scared to make public due to the ridicule and persecution you know you would receive if you did. This is the "you" God treasures. This is the "you" God loves. He loves this "you" so much He gave the ultimate sacrifice of His son to save you from sin, death and the grave. He gave so you and He can be together forever.

> *For God so loved the world, that* ***he gave*** *his only begotten Son, that whosoever believeth in him should not perish, but have everlasting life.* —John 3:16

God wants you to give not because He needs the money, but so He can brag about being loved by you as much as He loves you.

## Be Just Like Your Daddy

After realizing how much God loves us, it should move us to try to honor our Father by acting like Him. Although it is important to understand, through only sowing can one expect to reap a harvest of blessings, you should not sow just to reap. However, the purpose for your sowing is to honor God by reflecting His nature. You should not give just so your bills are paid, or to even become a millionaire. But you should give because it is the will and character of your Father.

Just consider what your life would be if you just tried to be more like our giving and loving God. Just think about how much more blessed your life would be if you took on His nature and committed to fully operating in this principle of sowing and reaping. What type of impact could your church make in your community, city, state and nation if you would just commit to developing a giving lifestyle?

There is no way around it. You reap what you sow! So do not expect to reap what you do not sow!! God rewards those who are willing to live with open hands. So make the choice to develop a giving lifestyle. I promise you that once you do, you will receive a harvest that is pressed down, shaken together to make room for more, and running over.

Be like your Daddy and start sowing today!!

Chapter 12

Kingdom Key #8

# *Release the Power of the Tithe*

# Chapter 12

## Kingdom Key #8

# *Release the Power of the Tithe*

> *Bring ye all the tithes into the storehouse, that there may be meat in mine house, and prove me now herewith, saith the LORD of hosts, if I will not open you the windows of heaven, and pour you out a blessing, that there shall not be room enough to receive it.* —Malachi 3:10

The previous chapter discussed the *Kingdom Key* of sowing and reaping. In this chapter we will address the specific principle of the tithe and why it is critical in developing and manifesting *wealth.*

The principle of tithing is taught within almost every facet of Christianity, and in most major religions in the world. Yet most people who consider themselves religious and/or a born again Christian are not totally committed to tithing. In 2002, George Barna of the Barna Research Group reported that although most Americans identified faith as a key factor in their life and considered themselves to be deeply spiritual, less than one out of every ten regular attendees of Christian churches gave 10 percent or more of their income – *a tithe* – to their church.[1]

This statistic is very disturbing because it reveals that most Christians do not perceive a value to the principle of tithing. This could be accredited to how the tithe has been presented from the standpoint of it being a duty or an obligation for the believer instead of it being the valued responsibility that comes with some very real spiritual and financial benefits. Sadly as a consequence, the majority of Christians in America will never experience these tremendous blessings due to their poor decision to not participate in this principle.

It is clear to me that if the people of God are to fulfill their God given destinies then they cannot afford to continue this trend of not tithing. Thus my assignment is to inspire you to start and/or continue to tithe by clearly describing the basics of the principle of the tithe and the benefits gained from tithing.

## The Basics

### *What Is The Tithe?*

The word tithe comes from the Hebrew word *"masser"* which literally means "a tenth". The word tithe equals ten. There are some people who may *say* that they give 15 percent tithes or 8 percent tithes, but this is impossible due to its very definition. For those who give more than the required 10 percent they are actually giving offerings to the Lord above their tithe. This is not a bad practice to have because of the principle of sowing and reaping that is associated with our offerings. However, for those who try to claim that they tithe based on a percentage below the tenth are not tithing at all, but are rather acting in disobedience. Unfortunately, for those who practice this may be hurting themselves more so than helping because of the consequences that come from disobeying God. So it is just better to be real about your giving. You either tithe or do not tithe.

The tithe is an ancient system before the law. There are some people who use the excuse they do not tithe because it is a Jewish law established in the Old Testament, but not in the New Testament. But there are clear examples of tithing prior to when Moses made tithing a law. Abraham tithed of all his increase to the high priest Melchizedek (see Genesis 14). Jacob is shown dedicating to God a tithe at Bethel (see Genesis 28:20-22). Many theologians agree the tree of knowledge in the Garden of Eden was the representation of a tithe because it was set apart for God. (see Genesis 2:17)

### *What Are We To Tithe From?*

The tithe is to come from any earnings or increase that is provided to you. This is supported in the Bible where it says,

> *"And all the tithe of the land, whether of the seed of the land, or of the fruit of the tree, is the Lord's, it is Holy unto the Lord."*—Leviticus 27:30

If you are wondering if this means you give from your gross income instead from your net income, you are correct. This also means that you should tithe from any increase that you are blessed with, meaning monetary gifts, money found, bonuses, raises and yes, even tax-refunds.

To help those who are having trouble with this part of the principle I suggest they should consider how they want to be blessed – on the net or on the gross? There are some Christians who would argue that being asked to live off of 90 percent of their income isn't fair because the money is all theirs. They worked hard for it and should be able to determine how much or how little to give to God. But whose money is it anyway? Don't we only get what God gives us? If God did not give us anything, what would we have? The Bible supports this in I Corinthians 10:26 where it says, *"the earth is the Lord's and the fullness thereof"*. Have you ever wondered how much life costs? If God wanted to, he could charge us rent for our time here or a fee for the air we breath. When you look at it from this perspective, 10 percent of everything is minuscule compared to what the Lord could demand from us.

### The Tithe Is Holy

If realizing God is due so much more than the 10 percent He asks for is not enough to settle the argument of giving the tithe, Leviticus reveals to us another unique reason to obey God's request.

*"And all the tithe of the land, whether of the seed of the land, or of the fruit of the tree, is the Lord's,* ***it is Holy unto the Lord.*** *"* —Leviticus 27:30

Not only is the tithe the Lord's, but it is also *Holy unto the Lord.* What does Holy mean? Well it is defined as being "separated unto God". Anything that belongs to God is considered Holy. In Romans, Paul helps us in understanding this term when he talks about how our relationship with God should be considered once we give our lives to him.

*I beseech you therefore, brethren, by the mercies of God, that ye present your bodies a living sacrifice,* ***holy****, acceptable unto God, which is your reasonable service.* —Romans 12:1

Just like God calls us Holy because we are His, He also calls the tithe Holy because they too are separated unto God. The tithe belongs to God.

I know the above seems a little redundant, but this is a critical component that needs to be understood about the tithe. Once God lays claim to something or someone it cannot be successfully used for any other purpose. Some of you may be wondering how this can be true when you use it all the time? Well, what you must realize is that this is a Kingdom principle. This means that although you are able to physically use the tithe in the natural, you will ultimately suffer the consequence of it in the spiritual realm because of your disobedience.

### *Where Do We Give The Tithe?*

There are those who believe you can give 10 percent to any charitable organization and it still is qualified as a tithe. However, the Bible tells us clearly where to give our tithe and why.

*Bring ye all the* ***tithes into the storehouse****, that there may be* ***meat in mine house...*** —Malachi 3:10a

The storehouse, in which the scripture refers to, is the local fellowship in which you are being spiritually fed. In essence, you ought to give to your church. Even though giving to a charitable organization, non-profit social-corporation, or to missions is admirable and noteworthy, it does not qualify as a tithe. Simply because it is not the place in which God ordained. His name is not on them. They are not separated for His purpose.

Then there is the question, "What about television ministries?" There are many television ministries who are credible and do a great work for the Lord by impacting millions. However, they are not qualified to receive your tithe if you are not a member of their ministry. It's like buying groceries for another house other than your own. Why provide the means for food at someplace else other than where you eat. With that said, I do believe in giving offerings to noteworthy ministries and nonprofit organizations and charities.

*The tithe should be given first, right off the top.*

There are those who have an issue with tithing because it is suppose to be given to the church that is under the stewardship of the pastor or priest. Unfortunately, the church has suffered from persons and churches that have betrayed the trust of the people by misusing the tithe. However, this is not an excuse to not tithe.

Tithing is not about you holding the pastor or church in check, but about having the faith to obey and trust God to ensure His will shall be done through your obedience. If the integrity of your leadership is in question, then you have every right to leave that church and find a leader and a fellowship in which you can trust the development of your faith.

### *When Do You Give The Tithe?*

The tithe should be given first, right off the top. It should be the first thing paid from your paycheck or from any increase that you receive. That's right, the tithe should be paid before you pay any bills like your mortgage, car payment, utilities, or groceries. I know this sounds crazy, but before you make this judgment let's look at the reasons why we should give our tithe before anything else.

The first reason why we should give the tithe first is probably the most basic to understand yet the most important to accept.

*Honour the LORD with thy substance, and with the firstfruits of all thine increase:*
—Proverbs 3:9

As we stated earlier, the very definition of the tithe is "a tenth". But this is not end of it. Although the tithe means ten percent, it is not just any ten percent, but the *first ten percent.* The tithe is the first fruit of your income. It is not the middle, or the next to the end fruit. It is not "if I have it fruit", or the left over fruit, but it is the first fruit. So, whenever you see the term first fruits, or anything referred to as a first thing, it is the same as a tithe. It is the same because it falls under the law of first things, which simply states all first things belong to God. This is His portion and His alone and is not to be touched by anyone or anything else. The tithe is the Lord's. This principle relates back to the tithe being holy. It is consecrated and devoted to God and Him only. God said it belongs to Him, which is why He demands it is given to Him first.

Proverbs 3:9 lets us know when you obey the word of the Lord by giving your tithe first unto the Lord, you *honor* God. You honor him through your obedience to God's Word and through the faith of your actions.

## A Matter of Faith

One common misconception about tithing is it is just a matter of money!! Yet, nothing could be more further from the truth. You see tithing is not a matter about money, but a matter of faith.

This is the second reason why you should tithe first, before doing anything else with your income. Because it's all about faith. Many people are under the misconception that tithing is all about the money so they give the tithe from what's leftover instead of off the top.

For example, say a person's gross weekly income is $500 per week. So the tithe is $50 per week (10 percent of their income). Instead of paying their tithes first, they go ahead and pay their bills (which is most likely the minimum payment), do some shopping and then take themselves out for a night on the town. This leaves them only $70 come Sunday morning. Remember their tithe is $50 for the week. If they pay their tithes, now, after having spent most of their money they will only have $20 left till the next payday.

As you can see, now this person has a huge decision to make. Do they give God that $50 and try to make it to the next payday on $20 or do they just decide to give God an offering for this week with the promise to do their "duty" later? Unfortunately, most people decide to do the later and only give a couple of dollars (if anything at all) promising to do better next time.

This is why God tells us to give the tithe first, because when you give off of what you have leftover it is not based off of faith, but off of fear. It is based off of fear because as you compare what you should give to what you have, fear and doubt sets in your mind and ultimately convinces you to rob God rather than to give unto Him.

If this person gave off the top, they would have had 90 percent ($450) of their money to work with rather than the 14 percent they had left over. This would have been considered giving by faith instead of by fear because by doing so they were showing they believed God would take care of their needs after they tithed. The only way you can do this is by faith.

God desires that we do everything in faith. In fact, God feels so strongly about this He considers any action done without faith a sin.

*". . .for whatsoever is not of faith is sin."*—Romans 14:23

Think about it, when you make the decision to not tithe you are committing a sin. Check this out. Even if you tithe, but it's after paying everything else off first you are *still* considered committing a sin. Why is it considered a sin? Because it is not *first!!* You are not showing you believe God will take care of your needs by your decision to not honor Him first.

Now, think about all of the sin that occurs every Sunday morning during tithes and offering time. Hopefully, this should disturb your spirit as much as it does mine. It also should explain why most churches are not experiencing the full glory of the Lord. The church has no power because of the constant sin that occurs weekly. No wonder God still desires true worshippers.

### *What Are The Benefits Of Tithing?*

Many Christians wonder if there are any benefits to tithing. The answer to this question is a resounding YES!! A tithing Christian is a prosperous Christian! This is so because the tithe is the foundation for divine prosperity in every area *(spirit, soul, body, finances and status)*. These blessings are clearly outlined in Malachi.

> *Bring ye all the tithes into the storehouse, that there may be meat in mine house, and prove me now herewith, saith the LORD of hosts, if I will not open you the windows of heaven, and pour you out a blessing, that there shall not be room enough to receive it.*
>
> *And I will rebuke the devourer for your sakes, and he shall not destroy the fruits of your ground; neither shall your vine cast her fruit before the time in the field, saith the LORD of hosts. And all nations shall call you blessed: for ye shall be a delightsome land, saith the LORD of hosts.* —Malachi 3:10–12

### *Open You The Windows Of Heaven*

The first blessing mentioned is the Lord's promise of opening you the windows of heaven. Now you may ask yourself what are the windows of heaven? The best way for me to describe this is to tell you about my present location. Although I pastor and live in Sacramento, California, I am often called upon to travel to various states for different conferences and other ministering opportunities. Recently, I went to Birmingham, Alabama. During that time of the year, the season called for the occasional thunderstorm. Unfortunately, the stormy weather caused a period of time where there was continuous overcast. When I looked out my hotel window, everything looked dreary and grey. It was dark and depressing because the clouds were blocking the rays of the sun. As I looked towards the sky I noticed my vision was limited and it was hard to see beyond the effects of the storm. The heavens were shut up!

Earlier, I saw a story on the local news about how this type of weather is affecting people in Birmingham. The reporter said some residents were experiencing feelings of depression because of the constant overcast. To combat this feeling, the reporter encouraged people to exercise, and to do things that would distract them from the lack of sunlight while they wait for a break in the weather. The reason the heavy anticipation for a break in the weather is because once it came people would start to feel better. After the break, spirits would be lifted. After the break, relief would come. After the break, everything would just seem to be better because light that was once hidden will shine upon their city. All they had to do was wait until a break came along to reveal an open heaven.

Think about how many times you found yourself in a stormy season in your life. You felt far away from God because of your dreary situation. You could not see a way out because of the overcast in your life. You prayed for the Lord to give you a break. Deliver you from the storm. You knew that you could get through it if He would just provide you a little light in your situation.

Now think about how you felt when God answered your prayers. What was your reaction when the heavens just suddenly opened? Was it relief, joy, happiness, or even inspiration? I am sure it was at least one of those. Immediately, you began to see a little more clearly because of the revelation of light shining upon you. Your vision became unlimited because no clouds were blocking your sight. You had your hope back. Your spirit was lifted and you knew you could make it.

This is the very promise God gives to those who are obedient to His command to tithe. He promised when we tithe He would keep the windows of heaven open over our lives. This is important to know because when you have an open heaven you always have access to hope. Hope is like that ray of sunshine that pierces through the clouds. It lets us know there is something better on the other side of the storm. This is why it is important to keep the window of heaven open because you need the hope that things are going to get better.

### *Pour You Out A Blessing That There Shall Not Be Room Enough To Receive It*

Once your window is open, God tells us He would pour you out a blessing. I don't know about you, but I have never heard of someone receiving a blessing from out of the sky. In fact, I am an avid tither and have never had a car, house or even money fall on me. So what does this promise really mean? What exactly does God pour out of heaven's open window? The answer to this question is *revelation*. Let me explain.

The reason the proud residents of Birmingham were anticipating a break in the weather is because of the feelings of hope that would spring from the discovery, or revelation, of clear sky on the other side. The feelings of hope and expectation are the same ones we feel when God opens a window over your life because of what He *reveals* to you about your destiny.

*When you tithe, you can expect God to give you divine insight on who you are and where you are to go.*

What is destiny? One definition of destiny is "the inner purpose of a life can be discovered and realized." Now check this out. If you look at the word destiny you see that it is a derivative of the word *destination*. The term "destination" is defined "as the place to which somebody or something is going or must go" and "a purpose for which somebody or something is intended." So the revelation of one's destiny is the realization of one's purpose that was once hidden.

When you tithe, you can expect God to give you divine insight on who you are and where you are to go. He will also reveal who has the resources to help fulfill your destiny. That's right, those who tithe will find out who has their stuff!! He'll let you know whose going to bless you. Who will give you that loan, give you the house, the car and the break that you need!! However, when you do not tithe, God will not show you anything.

All of this is exciting, but there's more to this promise for you. God said, *"I will pour you out a blessing, that there **shall not be room enough to receive it**."*(Malachi 3:10) That's right God is saying that He is ready to bless you *big time* so much so you will not be able to receive it all.

Of course you know our God is one of abundance. So it is in His nature to overwhelmingly bless us. But does this mean He is wasteful with His blessings? If not, why is God promising to bless us with more than what we can receive? Naturally this seems ridiculous, but let's look at it from a spiritual perspective.

The Bible tells us good men leave an inheritance to not only their children, but to their children's children as well (see Proverbs 13:22). In order to do this, one has to have a vision large enough to encompass his seed and their seed. Great vision is birthed out of great destiny. Only God can give you the blessing needed to have such a destiny that will prosper you, your children and their children. The tither is guaranteed such a blessing form the Lord. The blessing they receive is so vast it reaches beyond the tither to their grandchildren. You want to stop passing on generational curses? Then start tithing and start passing on a generational blessing. It will be the inheritance that will bless your grandchildren.

This promise to the tither is crucial for Christians to understand and embrace because it is the key in overcoming life's challenges and ultimately fulfilling our purpose of establishing God's Kingdom upon the earth. You have no chance of fulfilling your destiny by always being distracted by your current situation. You need to always have hope you can overcome any trial that life brings. Hope happens only when you know your present situation is not your final destination.

### *Rebuke The Devourer For Your Sakes*

I have a good friend who calls the tithe his "rebuke the devourer bill". He said he pays it so he can make sure that the devil cannot touch his stuff in any shape, form or fashion. After God blesses you with revelation of your destiny and starts to provide the resources to attain it, you can make sure you will need *divine protection.* Security of your destiny is needed because the enemy will do everything to try to spoil the fulfillment of it. Please understand Satan is not just going to hand over your destiny on a silver platter. But he is willing to do whatever it takes to destroy your future. In fact, Satan has a special spiritual assassin whose sole assignment is to totally annihilate any hope your destiny brings. So God promises the tither that He will protect them by rebuking this spiritual assassin called the devourer.

The word rebuke in Hebrew means to chide, to reprove, to agitate, to move out, to toss away, or to say, "stop it; that's enough." When you honor the Lord with your firstfruits, or your tithe, you are marking a place for God to fill in your life. You are giving God a place to stand between you and the devourer to rebuke him. Catch this. The only one who has the power to rebuke the devourer is God. The only way to get God to rebuke the devourer is through the giving of your tithe. If you do not honor God with your firstfruits, your tithe, then you have not given God a place in your life that He can fill. So when the devourer knocks on your door, God has no choice but to stand back and watch the assassin at work because you have not honored Him. If you do not make a place for God to rebuke him for your sake, then he has the right to take your stuff and devourer it!!

There are a whole lot of Christians dealing with problems that are totally avoidable if they just tithed. But because they have not made a place for God to stand and rebuke the devourer, they must endure situations that they shouldn't have to. I am sure you know of Christians who seem like they can never get ahead. It seems as soon as they get the promotion, their car breaks down. As soon as they get the bonus, their refrigerator stops working. As soon as they get one major bill paid, another one springs up. It's always one thing after another. Why? Because they have not paid their "rebuke the devourer bill". Consequently, the devourer has free reign to eat up their stuff.

My question for you... Are you paying your *rebuke the devourer bill*?

### *He Shall Not Destroy The Fruits Of Your Ground*

This promise is much more personal and intimate one than the other because it deals with our ground. The word ground in Hebrew is the word "adamah" which is the same word used in Genesis 2 where it says that God formed man out of the ground (adamah). This is where we get the name

"Adam" because he was taken out of the "adamah" or the ground. The Bible also states from dust you came; to dust you shall return. So one can derive when God speaks about the earth or any references to it like ground or soil, we can link it directly to man.

Proverbs 4:23 admonishes us to *"keep thy heart with all diligence; for out of it are the issues of life."* The condition of our ground or adamah is determined by the condition of our heart. Have not you met someone who you immediately determined they have a good heart? You formed this opinion about this person because of their pleasant demeanor. They always seem to conduct themselves in a friendly manner. These are the people whose perspective is the glass is always half-full instead of half empty. We like hanging around them because they make us feel good. Their joy is contagious. Plus, they are always looking out for someone else's best interest. Because of their good nature and kind spirit we determine they have a "good heart." The reason we believe this is because of the truth that whatever is on the inside will ultimately show up on the outside. If you are ugly on the inside, it does not matter how good-looking you are on the outside. Your ugliness will eventually come out. If you have a critical spirit it will manifest itself in your talk about others and so on and so on. It is critical to understand this impact that your heart has on your life.

To further explain this, let's look at when Jesus uses the parable of the sower. (see Mark 4:1-20) In it He talks about the sower sowing seed, which represents the Word of God, and how the condition of the soil affects the outcome of the sown seed. The parable states, some seed fell by the wayside and the fowls of the air came up and immediately devoured it. Some fell on stony ground, and immediately sprang up because it had no depth in the earth. The soil was shallow thus the seed could not take root. So although it grew, it was scorched by the sun and immediately withered away because its roots lacked depth. Seeds fell upon thorns, and the thorns grew up and choked it and it yielded no fruit. Finally some fell on good ground, and did yield fruit some thirty, sixty and some one hundredfold.

Like the disciples in the scripture, you may wonder what does this parable really mean. Remember, whenever you see God talking about soil or ground in the Bible, it represents the heart of man. The different types of soil represent the various conditions a man's heart can be in.

The first description of seeds falling by the wayside represented hearts resistant towards the Word of God. Due to the hardness of these hearts, the Word had no effect at all on them. So, instead of the Word taking root in their lives, it was left as seed by the wayside available for the enemy to consume at will. Those with this type of ground are incapable of producing fruit at all. No matter how much word they hear, they never grow or become better from it because of their total disregard for the word. Their hearts have grown cold to the word and left them bitter and barren.

The second description talked about those who have a heart to hear the word and even receive the word with gladness. However, when trouble comes into their lives they panic and lose hold of God's Word because the hearts were stony. Stony ground represents shallow ground. Unfortunately, in this type of soil a seed roots are not allowed to tunnel deep into the ground because of its lack of cultivation. The deeper the roots the stronger the plant. This soil represents those where the seed of the word does not take root in their lives due to their lack of maturity or trust in the Word of God. So at the first sign of trials they panic and give up because they have not accepted the Word of God at a deeper level in their lives.

The thorns depicted in the third description represent those who's hearts are obsessed with the cares of the world. Although they receive the Word of God with joy and gladness, it immediately gets crowded out by their fixation on attaining wealth and luxuries so much so they place it before God. God does not mind you having money or luxurious items. However, he does mind these things having you. It is only when we seek first the Kingdom of God that He promises all these things (money, earthly luxuries) will be added unto us. (see Matthew 6:33)

Finally, the good ground found in the final description represents a heart that is fertile. Not only willing to hear and accept the Word of God, but also ready to act on that Word in the manner that will produce a harvest in their lives that promises a return of thirty to sixty to one hundred of what was planted.

These are the people who always seem to be blessed no matter what state they're in. They are blessed during the good times and blessed during the bad times. They are the true examples of being prosperous, ruling their circumstances instead of them ruling you. Because their hearts are receptive to God's Word.

The revelation of this parable is the condition of the heart determines the type of effect the seed has in our lives. The problem is never the seed, but the ground in which it is sown. If your heart is hard, rocky, or crowded, you will never be fruitful in your life. But if your heart is found to be good soil, then the power of the word will *always* manifest in your life. This is why people can sit the same church and hear the same word, but never receive the *same* blessing.

*The revelation of this parable is the condition of the heart determines the type of effect the seed has in our lives.*

How do you keep the ground of your heart in good condition and know you will always be fruitful? ***Tithing.*** The Bible lets us know the preparations of the heart belong to man, but not totally to man. Jesus said, "I am the vine and my father is the husbandman." (John 15:1) We are the branches connected to the vine. We cannot produce fruit unless we stay connected to the vine through His Word. The husbandman is the one who is the caretaker of this whole process. He clears away any branches that does not bear fruit and prunes those so they may bear more fruit. How does He know which branches to discard and which to prune, by those who are receptive to God's Word. Those who are obedient.

I love preaching to tithers because they are not offended easily. Why? Because when the word comes to them, God, their personal cultivator, makes sure that the soil of their hearts is in prime condition to bear fruit. They know God's Word will *always* work in their lives and produce a harvest because of their obedience. No matter what they are going through. The tither has the promise to always have a harvest that is thirty, sixty or even one hundred times of the seed planted.

This is what it means when he says, *"he shall not destroy the fruit of your ground."* (Malachi 3:10) Only a tither has the guarantee that God becomes the husbandman, the dresser of their soil. He will stand between you and the devourer and say like the MC Hammer of old, "You can't touch this!"

### *Neither Shall Your Vine Cast Her Fruit Before The Time In The Field*

This fifth blessing concerns the issue of possession and time. The object of your possession is the fruit of your harvest. What God is promising the tither in this blessing is the absolute possession of your harvest. Once God says something is yours, you best believe that it is *yours!!* No one can take away what God says is yours. Tithers can be assured God has marked your blessing. So this leaves the issue of time.

Many believers become doubtful about the fulfillment of their blessing because of time. But to the tither, God is saying that delayed does not mean denied. The fulfillment of your blessing is not a matter of possession, but a matter of time. God's timing may not be your timing, but I guarantee you it is always the right timing. Your harvest will come right when you need it the most!! Not too early where it can be wasted, and not too late when it is of no use. But to the tither God promises that your guaranteed blessing will manifest itself in your life at His time. The right time. You will be in synch with God's timing. Always in step with the flow of the Lord.

### *All Nations Shall Call You Blessed, For Ye Shall Be A Delightsome Land*

Malachi finishes the list of blessings with,"*. . . and all nations shall call you blessed, for ye shall be a delightsome land.*" (Malachi 3:12) In other words, there will be evidence of a supernatural God on our side. How is this? Through the divine insight, provision, protection, and promotion resulting from tithing. Yet, it does not just stop there. God not only desires we possess spiritual evidence because of our obedience, but physical evidence as well. What does this mean? God plans for the Christian to have more than just a shout, jump or dance. But God desires His children also possess material blessings!! That's right. God wants you to have the "*bling, bling*" and the "*zing, zing*" so that people will wonder who you are, what you do, and who you do it for.

What I like about God is that He is *real!!* Especially in the sense of knowing the state of the world and what it esteems. It would be great if sinners were moved to accept God based on the vitality of our church services and the soundness of our doctrinal preaching. But the sad fact of the matter is nothing speaks success to the sinner than seeing someone materially blessed. God knew this during the Bible times, which is why he often blessed his servants with wealth. Since God does not change, we too have this opportunity to be blessed materially through our tithing. God's plan is for the Christian to have material blessings so that we can catch the interest of sinners by letting them know God is able to bless his children materially. The tithe is God's way of you having things instead of things having you.

### *Why Is The Tithe So Important To God?*

As you can see there are a number of blessings associated with tithing. The reason for this is, because of the great value God places on it. The tithe is important to God because of God's desire to prosper his people. In fact, His desire is so strong that God made covenant with Abraham to bless us. The tithe is a part of this covenant. Creflo Dollar calls the tithe the *"covenant connector"*, because it opens up the channel for God to bless and increase us in the manner in which He promised Abraham.

Abraham, or Abram as he was called at first, was called by God to come out of the place where he lived, a place called Ur of the Chaldees. God told Abraham He was going to bless him, make his name great, and that he was going to be a blessing. (see Genesis 12:1-3)

God also told Abram He would show him a land that He was going to give to him and his seed for an inheritance. God showed him the land of Canaan, the "promised land." Abram, his wife Sarai (as she was called then), and his nephew Lot, journeyed down to Egypt. Once there, an unusual thing happens. His wife Sarai, who was very beautiful, captures the interest of Pharaoh. So Abram, fearing for his life, gives Sarai to Pharaoh, claiming her as his sister *(she was in fact his half-sister)*. In return for her, Pharaoh gave Abram sheep, oxen, asses, servants, and camels. Abram receives so much stuff from

Pharaoh, he is considered wealthy. Pharaoh eventually finds out the truth, through a plague God sends. Eventually, God sends Abram, his wife, and Lot out of the country, leaving Abram with the wealth he gave him.

They journeyed back to the "land of promise" and the Bible goes on to state that Abram was very rich in cattle, silver, and in gold (see Genesis 13:2). There soon develops strife between Abram's herdsmen and Lot's herdsmen, and the two agree to go their separate ways. In Chapter 14:16, Lot and his household are taken captive as prisoners of war. When Abram hears about his nephew's situation, he decides to try to rescue Lot and his people. With three hundred men, Abram defeats the invading armies of four cities, rescues Lot and his people and rewarded with the spoils of war!! Abram was a bad man!!

After the battle, Abram meets a man named Melchizedek, who was a king and a priest. The Bible says he was without record of family ties, and no account of a beginning or an end (see Hebrews 10). Most theologians believe that Melchizedek was a type of Christ, if not Christ himself appearing in the Old Testament. While there Melchizedek blesses Abram and thanks God for his victory. In response, Abram, being a man of faith, gives tithes of his increase from the spoils of war to the high priest. He does this so only God receives the glory for his victory.

What makes this act so significant is that Abram does this out of his faith before any law on tithing was established. By tithing, Abram confirmed to God that he realized all of his blessings came from the Lord! Abram was just a steward of what God gave him. So it was only right to honor God by giving back to Him a *"tithe of all"* for his victory in battle. In response to Abram's faith, God expands His covenant with Abram to include his seed for generations to come.

> *And I will make my covenant between me and thee, and will multiply thee exceedingly. And Abram fell on his face: and God talked with him, saying, As for me, behold, my covenant is with thee, and thou shalt be a father of many nations. Neither shall thy name any more be called Abram, but thy name shall be Abraham; for a father of many nations have I made thee. And I will make thee exceeding fruitful, and I will make nations of thee, and kings shall come out of thee. And I will establish my covenant*

*between me and thee and thy seed after thee in their generations for an everlasting covenant, to be a God unto thee, and to thy seed after thee.* —Genesis 17:2-6

Galatians 3:29 says, *"If ye be Christ's, then are ye Abraham's seed, and heirs according to the promise."* Question. Are you saved? If so, you are Abraham's seed. This means you have the right to everything God promised Abraham. But here is the catch, in order for you to get your promise you have to act like an heir. How do you do this? By modeling after Abraham, the father of the faith.

Abraham proved to God he could stand to be blessed *big time* by tithing. Never did Abraham ever think his blessings resulted from his own hand. This is how the tithe connects us to the blessings of Abraham. When we tithe it shows we are like Abraham. Our tithing proves we understand that God is the source of every blessing that comes our way. Our tithing proves that, yes, even we can stand to be blessed *big time*!! This is why the tithe is important to God. It is His vehicle to keeping His covenant.

### *What Happens When I Do Not Tithe?*

When discussing the benefits and the importance of tithing, one cannot help but look at the disadvantages of not tithing. Just as the Bible is clear on the benefits of tithing, it is also clear on the consequences of not tithing.

*Will a man rob God? Yet ye have robbed me. But ye say, Wherein have we robbed thee? In tithes and offerings. Ye are cursed with a curse: for ye have robbed me, even this whole nation.* —Malachi 3:8-9

There is no question that churches are filled with people who do not tithe. There are many excuses given for not tithing. "I can't afford it." "I don't understand it." "I'm not ready now, maybe later." However, what is not understood is how by hiding behind these excuses affect your divine prosperity. Malachi 3:9 tells us when we rob God of our tithes and offerings; we are cursed with a curse. Before I talk about the curse, let me explain how we rob God.

Every promise in the Bible is conditional. Meaning that I have to meet a requirement in order for me to get what I want. Every act of disobedience sown will reap its own consequence. The result of being disobedient in the tithe is opening up our financial lives to the will of our enemy. We remove God's protection over our finances and *rob* God of His opportunity to bless us.

Another consequence of robbing God is the negative impact it has on your relationship with God. When you decide to not tithe, you are telling God you do not trust Him enough to supply your needs and bless you. You make yourself an idol by depending on your own strength rather than on the strength of the Lord. When you start doing this, your heart to God starts to turn cold and hardens to the point that you will not produce fruit. If you do not produce fruit, then you are of no use to God. God will not bless what He cannot use.

Furthermore, you rob the storehouse (church) of meat or resources needed to effectively perform ministry. Many within and outside of the church constantly criticize it for its lack of ministry in some shape or form. Yet, too often these same people who easily disparage the church never seem to tithe on a regular basis. This causes undue pressure and stress on the leadership of the church and literally cripples the body of Christ to the point of ineffectiveness.

## How To Tithe

So you have learned the basics of tithing. What the tithe is. Where to give your tithe and when you should give it. Then we explained the benefits of following this principle, which also revealed to us the innate dangers that we open ourselves to when we do not tithe.

So you have a better grasp on the concept of tithing and you really, really, really want to tithe. The only problem is the reality of your bank account. How can you afford to tithe? It seems like you are struggling to make ends meet now with what you make. You are deep in debt. Always paying the minimum on your credit cards. You struggle to put gas in your car? So how in the world are you going to find room in your budget to give 10 percent of yours to God? Please keep on reading, because I am going to show you how to apply what you have learned spiritually to your natural situation. Automatically.

## The Automatic Process

Remember how excited when you got your first job? If you were like me, you were thrilled about the prospect of making your own money and not having to rely so heavily upon mom and dad. Your first job was a milestone in your life because it showed you were no longer a child, but you were transitioning into adulthood. You were taking responsibility for yourself and your future. You were now finding out what it was like to be independent.

Now, remember when you received your first paycheck? Remember how shocked and disappointed you were when you found out for some strange reason the amount you received did not add up to the amount you agreed to. Again, if you were like me, all of my excitement of working went out the door. In fact, I just knew some giant mistake had been made. So I took myself down to the payroll department and demanded an explanation. Of course, to my embarrassment, this is where I received a crash course on the necessary evil of taxes.

For approximately sixty years the United States government has been utilizing a system to make sure that they will receive the taxes required from us to them. As you know, they do not wait for you to pay them after you receive your paycheck. Rather, they go ahead and take out what is due to them *first,* before we even get paid. How do they do this? Through an automated process called *electronic funds transfer* (EFT). As a result, the U.S government is pretty successful in collecting what is theirs. It also keeps a lot of people from having to experience the trouble of becoming delinquent on paying their taxes to the Internal Revenue Service (IRS). Believe me, this is a good thing, because you do not want to go up against the IRS.

The reason why the government takes out their taxes automatically is because they found out that they could not trust people to pay their taxes on the back end. Prior to 1943, people got their money when they earned it and was not asked to pay their income taxes until the next spring. However, this did not work out too well because the system was based on what the government *hoped* people would be, instead of the truth of what people really are.

The truth about most people is they are not money managers. People in general are too busy or just lack the discipline to budget, save or track our spending. *Just think about the last time you made a budget.* Consequently, most people do not know how much money they actually spend in a week, month or year.

Retail America doesn't help because they are always promoting us to spend every dollar that we have on the latest this or that. Then there is the prevailing attitude that if you do not have it, charge it. So now you are spending money that you do not even have. As a result, people are constantly surprised near the latter part of the month when their bank account tells them they have more month than money. So the government got smart and decided to change their system to accommodate who people really are by having you and I pay them first, then automating the process through electronic transfer.

*I believe the best way for God's people to pay their tithes and offerings is to do it automatically.*

As you are now aware, all types of banks and businesses now give us the option of paying for almost anything from the mortgage to basic cable - automatically. Why? Because it simply works. Although it doesn't totally take away the necessity of budgeting your money, it does simplify the process by making sure that you covered your necessities before you start spending money on your wants.

This system is so effective that it is now commonly used as a tool to enable people to build wealth by putting money away for their retirement and savings. This process even gives people the flexibility to conveniently put money aside for vacations, holidays and college tuition. **And again it works!!** It works because of the simple fact **you do not spend what you do not see!!**

Unfortunately, what corporate America and the U.S. government have known for years is now just being applied and accepted in churches. You may be wondering what I am implying so let me tell it to you straight. **I believe the best way for God's people to pay their tithes and offerings is to do it automatically.**

## The Automatic Tithe

For some of you who are reading this may be even more shocked than you were on your first payday. But consider the benefits of doing this. First of all, it gives you a system to obey the will of the Lord. I do not believe many of the advancements made in science, medicine, and technology was achieved for the benefit of sinners. Instead, these advancements are the children of God could better accomplish their purpose of establishing God's Kingdom on earth. What better way of accomplishing His will than by utilizing these systems of the twenty-first century?

Secondly, it is a method that keeps you in the position of receiving the benefits of the tithe. Many who claim that they tithe really are not tithers at all because of their lack of consistency. Thus they do not receive the benefits of tithing. Through tithing automatically you pretty much guarantee that you will be consistent in your giving. When you are consistent in your giving then you will be consistent in your receiving.

Thirdly, I believe God's favor those who take the time to plan their giving. When you decide to tithe automatically you are showing God His will is a priority in your life. This goes with the notion of being a cheerful and willing giver. This also shows God you have more faith of running over than fear of running out.

How do I know this works? Because my wife and I have been doing it for a number of years. Let me tell you, we have been blessed for it. God has shown so much favor in our lives financially because of us trusting enough in God to make him a priority. It has worked so well for us we introduced it to our membership. We call it the *Gideon Group*. God showed me that we could really do what we need to do with just 300 people dedicated to giving their tithes and offering automatically – and it works! Not only has the ministry been blessed, but those who stepped up to the challenge have also been blessed above and beyond what they can ask or think. In fact, many have had to increase their giving because of the blessings received from giving electronically. Again, when you make your tithing a priority, then God will make blessing you a priority.

### Tithing - Just Do it

Even after showing this system of paying your tithes, the reality is you must make the decision to do so. I have attempted to provide some much needed information about this *Kingdom Key* and how it is crucial to attaining *unlimited wealth*. Now it is up to you to decide to commit to doing it. Know that you will not reach the level of financial freedom you desire without doing it. Many in the world have discovered this fact and practice this principle because it simply works. Just imagine if it works for them, how it will work for you, God's child. No matter how you do it, make the decision now to make tithing apart of your worship lifestyle. Just do it. I guarantee once you do so, your future will be much brighter than your past.

## Chapter 13

The Master Key

# *Never Ever Give Up!!*

# Chapter 13

## The Master Key

# *Never Ever Give Up!!*

*And let us not be weary in well doing: for in due season we shall reap, if we faint not.* —Galatians 6:9

In this book I have shared with you certain *Kingdom Keys* that have opened up a wealth of opportunities and resources that have literally turned my dreams into reality and continues to do so. My intent in sharing these principles is so that you too can start to dream bigger dreams for your life and ultimately see them come to fruition. Yet, knowledge of these keys is only the start of the process of unlocking your treasure. Up to now you have been in the role of a student in my classroom. Your goal now is to strive to move from the level of an apprentice to that of a master so that one day you too may teach these keys to someone else. The only way to accomplish this is by following the advice that my father always shared with me. Advice that I have come to realize is the master key to all success. *Never Ever Give Up!!*

### The Power of Perseverance

Recently, I had the opportunity to see an interview of the well-known billionaire Donald Trump. One interesting thing to come out of this is how he faced financial ruin early on in his career. He was in debt for billions of dollars due to some projects going south for one reason or another. Consequently, the bankers who once eagerly chased him to do business with him now chased him to collect and cut ties. Seemingly overnight Donald Trump went from known as a brilliant business tycoon to the ultimate financial failure on the globe! Many thought this was the end for him, but it turned out it wasn't. As you may know, presently he is now more successful than ever being worth billions of dollars and the star and executive producer of the NBC television-hit show *The Apprentice.* The interviewer asked Donald how he was able to overcome that situation and become as successful as he is. And the Donald simply replied, "I never ever quit, I never gave up!"

Not quitting or not giving up is the best description of what it means to persevere. The power to persevere is your ability to continue towards your goals when you have every reason to quit! Success is not based on who's stronger, smarter, tougher, or better! But it is based on one's determination to push beyond every obstacle that comes their way and never ever give up! This is the secret to your success and the master key to unlocking your treasure!

Not giving up is more difficult than it appears on the surface. Proof of this is readily available in the form of the hundreds of thousands of people who has given up on the pursuit of their goals and dreams. Quitting is popular! The reason for this is because the act of quitting is more accepted in this day and age. Don't like your marriage? That's OK. Go ahead and get a divorce! Who cares how it affects your children, finances or future. Not happy because your boss won't let you take a two hour lunch break? Well you go ahead and show him or her who's the boss and quit and live off the system! Did not like what your Pastor preached last Sunday? Well here's what you do! Pack up your membership and leave, even though this is your fourth or fifth church you've been a member of in the last two years.

These examples may sound harsh, but are more true than not. Quitting is commonplace because it often provides quick fix that pacifies our feelings and emotions. Yet we are not aware on how our quick decisions affect others and us for the long term. The truth of the matter is that quitting is never the right or best solution to our problems. There is no honor in quitting because it tells others you cannot be trusted. You word is not your bond! Plus, by giving up too soon you may miss out on an opportunity that only presents itself by going through the process of facing whatever is challenging you. In essence, when you chose to quit, you chose to lose!

What challenges have you decided to give up on? Could it be you are about to miss out on that wonderful opportunity that you've been looking for because of your decision? Remember, the race is not given to the swift or the battle to the strong, but to the one who endures until the end! Having the resolve to never ever give up is critical to your success because it is the hallmark of what it means to be a winner!

## You Are A Winner!

Inside of you is a winner waiting to be released! How do I know? Well, first of all you're reading this book! But primarily, because God has placed inside each of us the innate desire to win! In essence, you were born to win and designed to succeed! You were created to be triumphant in all things! Sadly, many quit on their dreams too soon because they are unaware of this wonderful truth! But whether you know it or not, it is true nonetheless. You were built for success! You are destined to win!

Why is it important for you to understand this? Well it is because *Winners never quit and quitters never win!* As I stated before, when you chose to quit you chose to lose. To put it bluntly, quitters are losers! So if you are born a winner in the first place, you go against your winning nature by quitting! So in order to get you out of your losing streak we must help you remember how to win. The only way to do so is by taking on the qualities that make up winners! Those qualities are *passion, focus, strength and courage,* and finally *faith!*

### *Passion*

What you will find out on your journey is there are many ways to become rich and successful. However, most people do not do so because they aren't passionate about what they are doing. In other words, they do not love what they do! Winners succeed because they love what they are doing. And if you are to live a winning life then you to must be passionate about what you do.

Discovering your passion is so critical to winning because within it is your purpose. Your life's calling. What is so sad about most people is that they do not have any idea what their purpose or passion in life is. Thus, they go through life as zombies being bored and unfulfilled because they are unaware of their passion.

To make up for this, most make the mistake of allowing others to tell them what they should be doing in their life. The main reason why many aren't happy in their careers is because they have settled for a job that they been convinced into liking instead of pursuing dreams they're passionate about. They've settled for working for bosses they do not like and for companies whose products and or philosophies they do not use or agree with all because of a paycheck. This is why we have people trying to still find themselves and are going through mid-life crisis in their late thirties early forties because they just discovered they've been living a passionless life. Now they are willing to quit everything and everybody trying to redeem what they lost!

*When you love what you do, you are willing to endure any obstacle in order to see it succeed.*

When you love what you do, you are willing to endure any obstacle in order to see it succeed. Because of your passion for it, you will be able to bring all of your creative energy to it to develop solutions others cannot even fathom. One reason why I know my future is destined to be successful is because I am working in my passion as a leader of God's people. My most sincere desire is to see people come into the full knowledge of God and His Kingdom! I love empowering people and helping them discover their inner divine greatness. Nothing gets me more juiced than seeing a person realize their dreams and goals through the revelation and revolutionary power of God! Therefore, my future is secure and I expect total success in every area of my life because I am working my passion, my purpose and my calling!

What is it you are passionate about? Once you discover this you will be one step closer to living life as a winner!

### *Focus*

*"...the soul of the diligent shall be made rich."*—Proverbs 13:4b (NKJV)

Along with passion you will need to be able to keep your focus if you are to experience success in your life. Distractions will be thrown at you from every possible place to derail you from your goal. However, you must keep your focus on the prize no matter what. Always remember wherever your focus goes is where your power flows. Therefore, you should be stubborn with your attention while in pursuit of your goals. *Keep the main thing the main thing.* Do not allow good things of the world distract you from your Godly assignment! If not, you will fall into the sin of procrastination, which will develop into dissatisfaction, and depression because you could not stay focused enough to complete your goal.

There is a common expression that says, *"A jack of all trades masters none."* I am sure you know of a few people who may match this description. They know just enough of everything to get them by, however, they still struggle in life because they have not mastered anything.

Every person who has become super successful did so because they focused on becoming an expert, specialist or master within their particular field. Donald Trump is a master Real Estate Developer. Oprah Winfrey is a master Talk Show Hostess. Michael Jordan is a master Basketball Player, Tiger Woods is a Master Golfer, Venus and Serena Williams are master Tennis Players, and T.D. Jakes is a master Communicator and Motivator. Notice, none are masters or experts of everything! So if you are still trying to be all things to all men, then you have destined yourself for a life of struggle and just getting by. Since becoming an expert is key to becoming successful, then how do you go about doing so? Well I am glad you asked.

There is only one path to achieving a level of mastery in a particular discipline or field. That path is practice. The act of doing a particular activity or skill over and over again in order to develop a level of expertise in it. The key to becoming good at something is by repetitively doing an activity on a consistent basis. This is why musicians rehearse, athletes train and exercise, and businessmen apply certain principles daily so at the end of the day, they will be able to perform and /or compete at their best.

One of the most common misconceptions of practice is that it is limited to only certain areas of our lives or even to just certain people in our communities. Yet, nothing could be more further from the truth. We all are affected by the principle of practicing. Every outcome of our life is a result of how we practice living it. It really isn't as difficult to figure out why your life is a certain way. All you have to do is look at what you are doing each day, every day. In essence, what are your habits? The term habit is just another word for practice. You are the outcome of your habits or what you are practicing daily. If you aren't trying to master anything in your life then you probably have bad habits. A person with bad habits will produce bad results. However, a person who is focused on a clear goal will end up having good habits, which will produce good results.

As I've stated before, failure and success are not accidents. They are the results of the decisions that we choose and the activities that we do daily. So, what are you focusing on each day? Are your habits taking you towards your goals or are they moving you away from them?

### *Strength & Courage*

*And he gave Joshua the son of Nun a charge, and said, Be strong and of a good courage: for thou shalt bring the children of Israel into the land which I sware unto them: and I will be with thee.* —Deuteronomy 31:23

When Joshua and the children of Israel were about to go into the promise land after 40 years of wandering around in the desert God told them all they had to do was be strong and have courage and they will possess the land. Strength and courage are critical qualities you have to have on your journey to your promise land. You will need strength to fight off the weak moments come and you will need courage for when you become afraid. The truth of the matter is you will become weak and afraid more often than you think during your journey. You will experience these feelings because you will be attempting new things that are outside of your comfort zone. Many times you may feel you have no idea if you are making any progress at all as your dreams and goals are delayed. But you must remember delayed doesn't mean denied.

There is a saying that 80 percent of winning is accomplished by just showing up! This was true for Joshua and Israel at the city of Jericho. God told them if they just showed up at the city and walk around it for a couple of days they would be victorious! They didn't have to lift a finger or strain one muscle to win the battle. Are you catching the point here? Most of the battle is won just by getting to the place where you need to be for God to do his thing! All you got to do is show up and allow God to show out by handling the situation. Yet, to do so takes strength and courage to position you for victory!

### *Faith*

*Now faith is the substance of things hoped for and the evidence of things not seen.*
—Hebrews 11:1

*Passion, focus, strength and courage* lead to the final quality of a winner and most important one of all, which is *faith!* You cannot be a winner if you do not have it! When all else fails you must have faith. For it is the essence and proof of your hopes and dreams. It is your faith that will lead and guide you when you cannot physically see your way. Faith is the title deed to your dreams. Through it, you declare you believe and possess your goals now even though they have not materialized yet. Because of this you are able to allow patience to have it perfect work so you may be fully prepared for what God has in store for you.

The process of transforming your mindset from mediocre to a millionaire one is not easy. In fact, it is a very arduous and challenging undertaking because it requires that you go through a total life-change. Change of mind, body and soul. It is your very own *Extreme Make-Over!* The challenge of change is that it does not occur overnight, but is fulfilled over time. Often times this is longer and more difficult than you expect as you move from what is comfortable and familiar to uncharted waters. You will be tested and tempted to give up many times as obstacle after obstacle attempt to block your way.

People who you once considered friends will turn their backs on you and even attempt to stop your progress. They will question your judgment and ridicule your resolve as the results your looking for become more and more delayed. Then there are the resource challenges. It will seem like there's never enough money or people to get the job done. Every bank you try to get a loan from seems to deny your applications. It will make you believe you have "NO" stamped on your forehead. But this is when your faith must kick in!

*You just have to believe in what you see on the inside instead of what you see on the outside.*

The Bible tells us the only way for us to be successful on our journey we must walk by faith and not by sight (see 2 Corinthians 5:7)! Therefore, when adversities come your way, you cannot allow yourself to get discouraged. You just have to believe in what you see on the inside instead of what you see on the outside. For the truth resides in your vision and not your situation. For by faith we know the battle is already over and the promises of God are already "Yes" and "Amen." Faith gives us the ability to live in the *already*! Which means operating in the knowledge that every blessing God has for us is *already* done! For God already established it in the beginning of time. All He is looking for us to do is to earn it by faith! Faith is the currency that purchases our blessings!

> *And we know that all things work together for good to them that love God, to them who are the called according to his purpose.* —Romans 8:28

How can you push past every *no* that comes in your life! By understanding all things are working together for your ultimate victory! Every *no* you hear leads you one step closer to your Yes! This is the confidence of the believer who walks in faith! Knowing you are going to win no matter what because of the promise that God is working it out for your good!

How many *no's* are you willing to endure to get your blessings? Your answer is a quick indication of how strong your faith is and if you truly have what it takes to win!

## Living Life As An Overcomer

When you decide to operate out of your *passion* with determined *focus* and use *strength and courage* to tackle every obstacle by *faith,* you then are living your life as an overcomer! What is an overcomer? One who employs the master key! One who *Never Ever Gives Up!*

There is a lot of talk about being a survivor! In fact there is a great song called "I'm A Survivor" by the popular R&B girl group Destiny's Child! *I know you know it!* The song has a great message of continuing to live on in spite of all the odds against you. Though a great message, I believe that it is better to be an overcomer than a survivor! John tells us why in the prophetical record of Revelations.

*He that* ***overcometh*** *shall inherit all things.* —Revelations 21:7

What is it that distinguishes an overcomer from a survivor? The promise of reward! You can survive, but your only reward for it is your existence. Although not bad, God tells us we can actually have more than just our lives for our trouble. You and I can have our life *with rewards* if we choose to overcome! The spoils goes to the one who is willing to conquer, defeat, overpower and overwhelm every adversary and obstacle that tries to come between them and total victory!

Reality of your life's journey is it will be full of challenges and hardships that seem downright unfair! You will be betrayed, falsely accused, and set up to fail countless times all because of your dream! People you've loved and helped down the years and just knew would have your back when the going got rough, will turn on you right when you need them the most! You will experience pain, hurt, and disappointment. You will be tempted to become discouraged, depressed and to give it all up! It is right at these moments you will need to determine in your heart, mind and soul that you will overcome the temptation to quit and press on until you realize your goal!

## You Were Built For This!

During the funeral services for my father when it seemed like the weight of the world was upon me, my good friend and mentor, Rev. DJ Rogers Sr., grabbed me and looked me dead in the eye and told me, "You were built for this!" He said it again to me when my mother passed away nearly six years later!

Truthfully, I could point out to you a number of times when I have been tempted to call it quits and just let life run its course. I have certainly had enough tragedy and challenges in my life to justify it with the loss of both my parents and having to tackle the tremendous responsibility of pastoring my father's church at an early age. However, every time I start to think this way, I remember the words of DJ Rogers, which I have come to understand and accept over time – *You were built for this!*

*There is a millionaire on the inside of you waiting to be released in the world.*

Probably more times than not, you will feel as if your life is completely out of your control. You may even feel cheated because of the hand you've been dealt. And you wonder if you have any say in the outcome of your destiny. The first thing I need you to know is you are not alone. I have been there, thought, and felt it too! Yet, I have also learned these thoughts and feelings have no truth in them!

The truth of the matter is you do have control of your life and your future. Your destiny is a matter of choice and not of chance! There is a millionaire on the inside of you waiting to be released in the world. The key to doing so is in knowing *you were built for this!* Everything that has happened, is happening and will happen is a setup for your ultimate victory!

This is your time! You were born for this moment. You were chosen for such a time as this. You were uniquely created to do what God has challenged you to accomplish. Nobody else can fulfill the personal assignment God has chosen for you. You are called for this purpose! Everything you need is inside of you! There is infinite treasure in you! You are destiny's child!

So keep pressing towards the mark of your higher calling! And always remember to Never Ever Give Up! You got the keys, now it is up to you to use them! This is your moment. This is your time! Do not miss your opportunity to *Unlock Your Millionaire Mind!*

*For the race is not given to the swift or the battle to the strong, but to the one who endures until the end!*

—Dr. Tecoy M. Porter Sr.

# *Tribute to My Mentors*

As I mentioned earlier, a mentor is your closet thing to having a shortcut to success! As I reflect over my life, I realize that I have been privileged to receive many shortcuts from persons who thought me worthy of the investment of their time and wisdom. Therefore, I thought it well to place this tribute to them, my mentors, because of their significance and impact upon my life. I cannot express enough the level of my appreciation to each of you!

Dr. Robert and Hazel Porter

*My parents, who taught me how to be a son, a man, a leader, a husband, a father and finally a Pastor. Your memory lives on in your legacy!*

Deacon Lester and Martha McQuillon Sr.

*My in-laws (in-love), who teach me daily what true loyalty, love and respect is. Thanks for letting me marry your daughter! You are an awesome example of grandparents I plan to model after someday.*

Dewayne J. Rogers

*My spiritual father and friend! Every time I'm in your presence I am in school! I have learned and am learning so much from you. However, the greatest lesson I have learned from you is how to keep a promise! Thank you for keeping yours! Forever loyal to you!*

Bishop Samuel Williams

*My spiritual father from the East Coast! God placed us all together at just the right time and season of our lives. You have taught me love has no limits or boundaries. Thanks for taking us in! You are the greatest!*

Bishop T. D. Bishop Jakes

*My Pastor, you have unknowingly done for me what you have done for so many others by healing the brokenness in my life. Your words and life are truly an inspiration. You have shown me what it takes to truly lead God's people in the Twenty-first century.*

Pat Kava

*My former supervisor and friend from the University of California, Davis. You taught me how to become a strong leader in a corporate setting. Thanks for taking a risk on me by giving me the opportunity to develop my skills under your supervision. Your training helped prepare me for my position as a Pastor.*

Jackie Ward

*You were the first music executive to sign us to your independent label – Noah's Ark Music, Inc. Introduced us to the gospel music industry and taught me the ins and outs of it. Thanks for the start! I will never forget it.*

Marion Kennon

*My unofficial guidance counselor from 7th – 12th grade at Breck School in Minnesota. You taught me, an urban black middle class kid, how to adapt to the super rich kids and community my school served. Thanks for getting me the scholarship and never making feel like I was on one!*

The following are my musical mentors. Each of them significantly stirred up the gift of music in me in one form or fashion and I am truly grateful for their time and instruction.

Rev. Carl Walker
*(Walker West Music Academy, St. Paul, Minnesota)*

Lisa Doering
*(Breck School, Golden Valley, Minnesota)*

William Dehning
*(University of the Pacific, Conservatory of Music, Stockton, California)*

Claudia Kitka, Donald Kendrick
*(California State University, Sacramento)*

Clarence Eggleton, Bobby Adams, and Frank Fenner
*(Genesis Baptist Church, Sacramento, California)*

# *Citations – End Notes*

Chapter 4

1. Tracy, Brian. *Focal Point: a proven system to simplify your life, double your productivity, and achieve all your goals.* New York: AMACOM, a division of American Management Association, 2002

2. Hansen, Mark Victor. and Robert G. Allen. *The One Minute Millionaire: the enlightened way to wealth.* New York: Harmony Books, 2002

Chapter 5

1. Bishaw, Alemayehu and John Iceland. *Census 2000 Brief - Poverty: 1999,* U.S. Census Bureau, issued May 2003. http://www.census.gov/prod/2003pubs/c2kbr-19.pdf. (accessed January 2006)

Chapter 10

1. Maxwell, John C. *The 17 Indisputable Laws of Teamwork: embrace them and empower your team.* Tennessee: Thomas Nelson, Inc., 2001

Chapter 13

1. Barna, George. http://www.barna.org. The Barna Group, Ltd. 2006